MANAGEMENT OF MARKETING COMMUNICATION AND ADVERTISING

MS-68

Notes For

Master of Busines Administration [MBA]

Useful For

IGNOU, KSOU (Karnataka), Bihar University (Muzaffarpur), Nalanda University, Jamia Millia Islamia, Vardhman Mahaveer Open University (Kota), Uttarakhand Open University, Kurukshetra University, Seva Sadan's College of Education (Maharashtra), Lalit Narayan Mithila University, Andhra University, Pt. Sunderlal Sharma (Open) University (Bilaspur), Annamalai University, Bangalore University, Bharathiar University, Bharathidasan University, HP University, Centre for distance and open learning, Kakatiya University (Andhra Pradesh), KOU (Rajasthan), MPBOU (MP), MDU (Haryana), Punjab University, Tamilnadu Open University, Sri Padmavati Mahila Visvavidyalayam (Andhra Pradesh), Sri Venkateswara University (Andhra Pradesh), UCSDE (Kerala), University of Jammu, YCMOU, Rajasthan University, UPRTOU, Kalyani University, Banaras Hindu University (BHU) and all other Indian Universities.

GullyBaba Publishing House Pvt. Ltd.

ISO 9001 & ISO 14001 CERTIFIED CO.

Regd. Office:
2525/193, 1st Floor, Onkar Nagar-A,
Tri Nagar, Delhi-110035
(From Kanhaiya Nagar Metro Station Towards Old Bus Stand)
Call: 9991112299, 9312235086
WhatsApp: 9350849407

Branch Office:
1A/2A, 20, Hari Sadan,
Ansari Road, Daryaganj,
New Delhi-110002
Ph.011-45794768
Call & WhatsApp:
8130521616, 8130511234

E-mail: hello@gullybaba.com, **Website:** GullyBaba.com

New Edition

Price: ₹200/-

Author: Gullybaba.com Panel

Copyright© with Publisher

All rights are reserved. No part of this publication may be reproduced or stored in a retrieval system or transmitted in any form or by any means; electronic, mechanical, photocopying, recording or otherwise, without the written permission of the copyright holder.

Disclaimer

Although the author and publisher have made every effort to ensure that the information in this notes is correct, the author and publisher do not assume and hereby disclaim any liability to any party for any loss, damage, or disruption caused by errors or omissions, whether such errors or omissions result from negligence, accident, or any other cause.

If you find any kind of error, please let us know and get reward and or the new notes free of cost.

The notes is based on IGNOU syllabus. This is only a sample. The notes/author/publisher does not impose any guarantee or claim for full marks or to be passed in exam. You are advised only to understand the contents with the help of this notes and answer in your words.

All disputes with respect to this publication shall be subject to the jurisdiction of the Courts, Tribunals and Forums of New Delhi, India only.

About Publisher

Gullybaba Publishing House is the brainchild of Mr Dinesh Verma, his name alone evokes profound respect and admiration. He is the pioneer of providing quality materials to the students of IGNOU because, having been a student of IGNOU, he understood the difficulty and pain of the non-availability of quality materials himself. He is serving the students with the following services:

EXAM-SUCCESS GUIDES
Important questions, solved question papers, guess papers - all in one! to score good marks in lesser time and effort.

FREE BOOK
As our love and care for our students, here is a Free Gift – A Famous Book "Secrets to Pass IGNOU Exams with Less Study" for you. You can download it now! https://www.gullybaba.com/ignou-free/

YOUR CONTRIBUTION TO MOTHER-EARTH
When you read our books, you save our mother earth as we use recycled paper to make these books. On every purchase, we contribute something to plant a plant.

SOLVED ASSIGNMENTS PDFs / HAND-WRITTEN
Best and genuine solved assignments PDFs you can instantly download from Gullybaba.com or our App.

PROJECT REPORTS/SYNOPSIS
Best Quality No-Rejection projects/synopsis by professionals researchers in ready to refer format.

MOBILE APP
You can download 'Gullybaba' app from Google Play Store to enjoy all above services at one place.

Why Gullybaba's IGNOU Help Books

Is Fear of Exams making you stressful? Are you not getting good marks in your IGNOU exams? Are you looking for sure-shot solution get ahead in your IGNOU studies? Look no further than the answer: Gullybaba.com! With our expertly crafted course help-books, you'll be ready to face any exam with ease-guaranteed. What's more, we offer a huge discount on IGNOU Help Books Combo Deals – Save BIG.

Now, complete IGNOU courses more quickly and with Good Marks in Lesser Time & Effort.

Home Delivery of GPH Books

You can order Gullybaba Books online from Gullybaba.com or Gullybaba App. We dispatch books on the same day of receiving the order through our fastest courier partners.

You can also order books through WhatsApp on 9350849407 or by email at order@gullybaba.com.

We also provide "Cash On Delivery" through our courier partners and sometimes Govt. Postal Department.

Important Note to Sellers

Selling this book on any online platform like Amazon, Flipkart, Shopclues, Rediff, etc. without prior written permission of the publisher is prohibited and hence any sales by the SELLER will be termed as ILLEGAL SALE of GPH Books which will attract strict legal action against the offender.

Notable Information

An attempt has been carefully made to present this book more useful and meet the requirement and challenges of the course prescribed by IGNOU University. We hope that this effort will fulfil the readers' expectations and help them excel in exams. Referring to University study material alongside this book is like "icing on the cake".

We wish you a successful and rewarding career. If you have any feedback to improve our books/products, please email at feedback@gullybaba.com. Because we believe, "Feedback is breakfast of champions" and our readers are our strength.

Table of Contents

Block-1 Marketing Communication and Advertising—Basic Concepts
Unit-1   Marketing Communication Process..1
Unit-2   Communication-Key Behavioural Concepts................................7
Unit-3   Indian Media Scene..13

Block-2 Advertising Campaign Planning and Execution
Unit-4   Planning Communication Strategy..19
Unit-5   Advertising Campaign Planning-Strategic
         Consideration, Creative Consideration...23
Unit-6   Advertising Creativity Campaign Planning and Execution.....31
Unit-7   Advertising Research - Role and Trends
Unit-8   Measuring Advertising Effectiveness Definitions and
         Techniques...49

Block-3 Media Planning Concepts
Unit-9   Media Concepts, Characteristics and Issues
         in Media Planning..55
Unit-10 Media Selection, Planning and Scheduling.................................61
Unit-11 Internets as an Emerging Advertising Medium.........................67

Block-4 Marketing Communication Form
Unit-12 Managing Sales Promotion..71
Unit-13 Direct Marketing...75
Unit-14 Publicity and Public Relations...81
Unit-15 Social Marketing Communication..85

Block-5 Strategies for Advertising Agencies
Unit-16 Functions and Structure of Ad Agency...87
Unit-17 Managing Client Agency Relationships..97
Unit-18 Strategies for Account Management...105
Unit-19 Legal and Ethical Issues in Advertising......................................114

Question Papers

(1) June-2020...125
(2) December-2020...127
(3) June-2021...129
(4) December-2021...131

Chapter-1

Marketing Communication Process

Q1. What is the role of marketing communication? And what are their concepts?

Ans. Marketing is a process of developing and exchanging, ideas, goods and services with the mutual consent of the two parties (buyer and seller). Marketing communication is a component of marketing mix 4 P's known as promotion. Marketing communication is nothing but a way of promoting product and services to the desired customer. The concept of marketing communication is to attract customer at macro and micro level, it means it can fulfill the need of both consumer market and industrial market, communication should be both sided, there must be sending of the feedback from the customer side. In this cut-throat competitive environment it becomes very essential for the marketing communication department, to communicate with the customer very quickly and effectively.

Information sending is not only the motto of it; there are various roles of the marketing communication, such as Inform: Provide the detail information about the product and services in which the organisation is dealing. Remind: It means to inform about the old product and services which have transformed or added a valued. And the last is to Persuade it actually works as a influencer for the targeted or the potential customer, it generally generate the need in the customers mind.

Marketer work in a dyad form, likewise: Communication in Marketer-Buyer Dyad (here dyad means to link a pair), the communication should be in such a manner so that each of them can understand the motive of the conversation. For an example if a company hires a sales person he/she should be matched to the customer, so that the interaction can increased, that's why in the demography, company try to hire the local candidates as their employee so that it becomes easy to understand their customer.

Communication in Marketer-Market Dyad: Here communication is not for the mass audience, but for the specific one. If an organisation deals in a specific product, than there will be the limited or ultimate buyer of that particular product and for them there should be a different message for each of them. For an example, company produce the cotton, its customer can be the Chemist, General Merchant, etc. so for each of them there should be different message.

Communication in Non-Profit/Social Organisation: For such organisation communication is an important part because wrong communication can spoil the image of the organisation and gives the bad impression to the public.

Q2. Explain the components of Marketing Communication Process?
Or
Define the elements of Marketing Communication Process?

Ans. In general the communication means the transfer of ideas, thoughts, feelings etc. from one person to another, and in this two things are mainly required that is source and destination, as when we talk about marketing communication professionally same things required, likewise here source means organisation and destination means the audience (customer).

However from sending to receiving the message there are various elements which an organisation has to take care because there is not only two person, but a huge audience and the image of the organisation which can be fall if the wrong message has been communicated to the wrong audience at the wrong place and time. So for correct message transferring one has to take care of the following elements:-

- **Source:** The sender of the message is known as a source of communication. The process starts when the individual, group of individuals or an organisation wants to communicate message to the targeted audience. Communication can take place in many ways ranging from face-to-face communication to electronic and print media.

  The essential thing which the sender has to ensure that the message which is sent to the receiver is perceived in the same manner as the sender perceived, because the perception of the receiver can be different from the sender, however the perception of the sender and receiver should be match, because the wrongly perceived message may result the failure of a product despite, it being superior in terms of features and quality.

- **Encoding Process:** It is a process in which the selection of the information is to be done. The sender has to ensure that the right amount of information is communicated to the receiver. Too much information may confuse the receiver and too little may not serve the senders purpose in communicating it.

- **Medium of Transmission:** It is the interface between the sender and the receiver or we can say it is a transporter of information from the source to the receiver's destination. Organisation selects the medium of communication on the basis of the information, targeted audiences, speed of the medium etc. Transmission of information can be done through different channels (medium) like personal (face-to-face interaction, telephonic conversation, communicating through mailer, e-mails, mobile messages etc. in which message can be customise according to the customer tastes and preferences) and non-personal(electronic media, print media and outdoor advertising) channels.

- **Decoding Process:** It is a process in which the receiver interprets the information that has been sent by the sender. The decoding becomes successful only when the receiver interprets the message with the same perception of the sender.

- **Receiver:** It is a place where the message has to be transmitted by sender. On the other hand it is only receiver who makes the sender's message successful or failure, so one has to be very careful about the receiver and before choosing the message or medium of transmission the sender has to choose the receiver.

- **Feedback:** It is a very essential step of the process, because it helps both the sender and the receiver for the consistent flow of the communication process. It helps in rescuing the problems or misunderstanding which is caused by the wrong interpretation of the message, and the sender can take the necessary action if it is required.

Q3. Write down the reasons through which the communication can be fail.

Ans. To run a company with the brand image, in this cut throat competitive environment, the flow of information regarding company must be precise and good, for this the marketing department has to take care before releasing any information about the organisation. The sources which can create the misunderstanding are as follows.

- **Source Effect:** As we know that the sender is the key step in the communication process, because he is only one who decide what to communicate when to communicate, where to communicate and to whom communicate. Incorrect, immoral selection of message can also spoil the good brand image of the company. In this the past image of the company matter a lot because the receiver perceives according to that only, bad reputation can harm the future of the organisation and it becomes more challenging to gain customer attraction again.

- **Multiple Transmitters:** The medium available in this technological era are very advance and huge in variety through which the message can be transmitted, so it becomes more important to select the right channel for message transferring, likewise if message can be transfer through personal channel one should be very careful for using the no-personal method for it.

- **Decoding Process:** When message is send to wrong audience it is definitely be interpret wrongly, likewise if the audience is niche then exclusive advertisement is waste, even if the company is producing a niche product.

- **Noise:** It is a hurdle or a barrier at the time of coding, transmission, decoding and feedback. It disturbs the intended message, which therefore may not be perceived by the receiver accurately. Noise can be technical defect, physical, social and psychological noise. Technical defect: - if the message is transfer through the mailer and it cannot be downloaded at the receiver end then the half message can give the inappropriate meaning of it. Physical noise: - if the message is transmitted through television and you are disturbed by the people sitting around. Social noise: - like if the protest is going on and the full coverage is not telecast by the news channels may caused the social imbalance. Psychological noise:- occurs when the emotional state of the individual is disturb like if the hair dresser cut the wrong cutting then the customer will not listen to the barber for any excuse.

- **Inappropriate Feedback:** To make communication process successful the feedback should be appropriate, company spends lot of budget on marketing their products and opt different-different strategies to achieve the customer loyalty and response. Poor and wrong feedback can misguide the company marketing research department, on the behalf of the feedback company process further. So, to be safe side most of the organisation spent lot of money and monitor to get the right feedback.

So, marketing department must have taken care of all the above listed points, so that they can do an effective and error free communication between the customer and the company.

Q4. Define the elements of Marketing Promotion Mix.
Or
What are the various tools of Marketing Promotion Mix?

Ans. Promotion is all about the communication, the word promotion is originated from the Latin word 'pro' which means forward and 'movere' means to push, thus, promotion means to push forward, this is a word which is extensively used in the marketing communication process, because it helps the organisation in achieving the targets. There are various promotional tools which are widely used by the organisation and it's a duty of the marketing department to choose the most effective promotional tools. Promotional tools can help the organisation in many ways like:- Increasing sales, attracting new customer, encourage customer loyalty, encourage trial, create awareness, inform customer, remind potential customer reassure new customer, change attitudes, create image, position a product, encourage brand switching and to support a distribution channel. The various promotional tools are as follows:

- **Advertising:** It can be done through print, electronic and outdoor media. It is a paid form of non personal presentation of product (can be goods or service) by an identified sponsor. The major advantage of advertising is that it can reach a large audience at a very low cost and firm can choose its targeted audience. Organisation can have their own in-house advertisement department or they can hire an advertising agency.

- **Sales Promotion:** Coupons, discounts, rebates, samples, offering various benefits in the form of incentives or by adding value to the products are the different ways of the sales promotion. Organisations try to spend more money on sales promotion rather than spending on the advertising. It is basically used to enhance the sale of the product or create the awareness about the product. For an example: - Free sachet of shampoo in the news paper.

- **Publicity:** It is a non-paid form of communication, which can be done by both print and electronic media. Publicity can be done by word-of mouth like if anybody like the product very much he/she will recommend or influence to other about the product. Publicity in non-paid form communication to understand this we can have the example of Facebook.com, it is getting publicity free of cost because company is not paying to get promoted in the market, only the customer, with the help of word-of- mouth promoting it.

- **Public Relations:** It is totally different form of promotion tool; it informs and educates the public about its activities, working and philosophy of the organisation. Now days organisations have their own public relation departments, organisation thinks that advertising can be supplemented by the PR. Organisation can develop its public relation with several member groups such as suppliers, customers, employees, the government, shareholders, distributors, member of the public etc.

- **Personal Selling:** Face-to-face interaction is known as personal selling, in this the sales salesperson has to personally meet with every potential customer. Although it is very expensive form of promotion but company gets immediate and accurate feedback about the product or services. For an example: Eurekaforbes (leading marketers and service provider of water purifier, vacuum cleaners etc.)

- **Direct Marketing:** Through this company can directly deals with the customer. In the present scenario it is a popular form of marketing, which is done through electronic media like internet, mailer, telephone etc. It is highly cost effective; through this we can deal with both customer and industrial market. For an example: Oriflame (Online shopping portal).

❏❏❏

Chapter-2

Communication-key Behavioural Concepts

Q1. It is important for the marketers to identify the customer needs and motivate them to make the product successful. Explain it.

Ans. Motivation is one of the vital factors in the consumer buying decision process. The motivation to fulfill needs is the key factor in the purchasing process. There are two kinds of need- primary 'physiological' needs and the second one is 'psychological' needs. The hierarchy of need is introduce by Abraham Maslow and is widely accepted by motivational theory. According to this theory, there are five levels:- physiological needs, safety need, social need, self-esteem need, and self actualisation needs. This theory explains that an individual struggles to fulfill basic need like hunger, thirst, etc. which are essential for survival. Motivation has a dynamic nature because existing needs are never fully satisfied, new needs emerge as old needs attain satisfaction and selection of goals is strongly affected by success/failure in prior goal attainment. Advertising as a function makes extensive use of the concepts of consumer needs and motivation in basically two ways. The first is the positioning application where the marketing communication is designed in response to whether the product is able to position to satisfy social needs, which can further fulfill the rational and emotional motives of the customer. The second one is less in use, in which advertiser try to understand the nature of advertising itself, so that they can prepare the marketing communication accordingly in response to the need.

Q2. What is consumer personality and psychographic?

Ans. Personality describes the psychology and behavior of an individual. It tells how an individual perceives himself or wants other to perceive him. It is believed those customers are influenced by their own self-image in different situation. The personality defines the self-image of an individual which are as follows:

- **Actual self-image:** It is how individual perceive themselves.
- **Ideal self-image:** It is how individuals would like to see themselves.
- **Actual social-image:** It is how individual are perceived by other.
- **Ideal social-image:** It is how individual would like other to see them.

Psychographics is a study of individual personal characteristics like activities, interest, opinion, values and lifestyle. Psychographic segmentation enables the advertiser to segment the whole population into 8-10 lifestyle type. A persons attitude is a set of feelings and the way in which he reacts to a given idea or thought. Attitude can be positive, negative or neutral. Customer's attitudes and beliefs influence his perception and buying behavior. It is based on their past experiences with the products and through their interaction and relationship with their respective reference group. Culture is considered as a set of rules, values, beliefs, behavior and concepts that is common and binds together the member of a society. Thus an individual buying pattern is largely influenced by the culture.

Q3. Does consumer perception works in buying decision process?

Ans. An individual processes the information captured and gathered from the environment, which frames his/her perception. The perception of the individual has a major influence on their buying decision process. For example a person may have the perception that widely advertised product are quality products. In result, person unconsciously prefers to purchase only well advertised product. However, the person's perception may not be true in all cases. A product may not be well advertise but may be high quality. Therefore perception plays a vital role in the consumer buying process. Few more perpetual processes consist of:

- **Selective exposure:** The interpretation of the message is an uncontrollable factor for the marketer. An individual could distort the message communicated by the marketers based on his/her beliefs or perception. The selective distortion makes it difficult for the marketers to communicate their desired message. The perception of the individual thus influenced the interpretation of the message. It may also result in the individual accepting only those messages that conform with his/her preconceived notions.

- **Selective attention:** The environment around an individual provides constant information. The individual is bombarded with various stimuli or message from various media. However he/she focuses on only a few things that catch his/her attention. This is known as selective attention. Marketers should try to win this focused attention of the customer, by using unique marketing strategy which is easy to recall.
- **Perceptual Defence and Perpetual Blocking:** After the marketers has communicated the message and the individual has interpreted it, the individual may not remember it for long. All the messages received may not be remembered. Therefore, marketers should try and make the message such that people will be able to retain and recall it. For an example Bournvita is famous for its "Tayyari jeet ki!" (Preparing to win) campaign.

Q4. How learning works in purchasing & consumption?

Ans. Consumer learning is the process through which individuals acquire the purchase and consumption knowledge and experience they apply to future related behavior. Advertising helps for marketers in generating need and for customer advertise helps to get knowledge and motivate them to make purchase to fulfill their needs. Thus advertising plays a major role in learning of the customer. Some important learning theory concepts of relevance to advertiser are as follows:

(1) Repetition: It is important to increase the likelihood and retention of the customer towards the product. Advertising schedules makes use of the repetition concepts in order to work out the necessary reinforcement needed for adequate retention, the repetition is important so that the association is remembered by the subject. Of course, too much repetition can also be a problem. Think of the ad you have just seen so many times you feel like you can't stand to see it again. This is known as advertising wearout which can be a big problem for advertisers, that is why they change their ads frequently.

(2) Stimulus generation: It is a process in which the advertiser uses the same background music, logo word or phraseology with the new product, so that the customer can recognise them that it belongs to their favorite brand. Only repetition doesn't work in learning, there should be generalise way to make learn customer about the product which can be done by stimulus generalisation, it is a theory in which, when a consumer applies a conditioned response to a stimulus that is not the same but is similar to conditioned stimuli. An example you might recognise is when we react to someone in a certain way because they remind us of someone we know and have interacted with before. Stimulus generalisation can be helpful as marketers extend their product line, product form, and product category.

(3) **Stimulus discrimination:** In the cut throat competitive environment every firms want the preference in the eye of the customer, so unlike stimulus generalisation the advertiser use the theory of stimulus discrimination. Stimulus discrimination is closely linked to the concept of positioning. Marketers want you to think of their product differently than the rest when you are looking at the other brands in the stores

The above written theory comes under behavioral learning theories of classical conditioning. Now the second one is cognitive learning which focuses on problem solving and consumer thinking. It is closely tied to information processing and how consumers store, retain, and retrieve information.

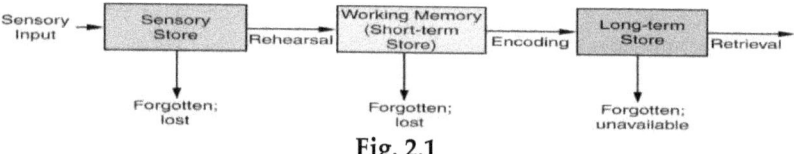

Fig. 2.1

In this process there are three places where a consumer will store information before processing. The sensory store is very short term; it is where an image or sound will last for just a few minutes and then be forgotten. The short-term store is the stage where information is processed. Similarly to the sensory store, it is just held for a brief time. Information will move, through encoding, to the long-term store. Information here can last for relatively extended periods of time.

Rehearsal, encoding, and retrieval play an important role in moving information from one place to the next. Rehearsal can be done either by repeating the information or relating it to other data. If held long enough, the information can be encoded, or given a word or visual image to represent the object. Finally, retrieval, the last stage of this process, describes how one can recover information. Situational cues are the most common reason to retrieve information.

Q5. How consumer attitude can be change through advertising?

A persons attitude is a set of feelings and the way in which he reacts to a given idea or thought. Attitude can be positive, negative or neutral. Customer's attitudes and beliefs influence his perception and buying behavior. It is based on their past experiences with the products and through their interaction and relationship with their respective reference group. Customer attitudes can have a major impact on firms marketing efforts. Therefore marketers must try to adjust their marketing mix to counter neutral and negative attitude of the customer.

Marketers can use several methods like observation, personal interview and direct questionnaires to study the attitude of the customer. Advertising which contributes to the learning inputs becomes a factor in attitude formation and its change. By using rational and emotional appeals advertisers try to contributes to the cognitive affective and the conative component of attitude.

Q6. Group influence in consumer buying behavior, explain.

Ans. Family, friends, formal social groups, colleagues at work and consumer action groups influence the consumers buying behavior significantly. An individual's family, great influence the buying patterns of the individuals. Subsequently, friends are the next important social group that influences the buying behavior of the individual. A friendship group is an informal and unstructured group. The influence of this group is significant on individual buying process, because things that are not normally discussed with the family members are discussed with friends. Formal social, groups like lion's club, etc do influence the individual buying behavior. The member in such group influences other members during informal discussions or by becoming a role model to other model to other member. During the working hours, an individual normally has formal and informal discussion with other employees and therefore, there exist an ample opportunity for influencing the buying behavior of the individual. These social groups influence buyers to refrain from buying those goods and services that exploit customer vulnerabilities.

❑❑❑

Must Read — अवश्य पढ़ें

G Gullybaba.com

GULLYBABA PUBLISHING HOUSE PVT. LTD.

New Syllabus Based

100% Guidance for IGNOU EXAM

IGNOU HELP BOOKS

BAG, BCOMG, BA (Hons.), BSCG, BSC (Hons.) B.A., B.Com., M.A. M.Com., BED, BCA, MCA and many more...

IAS, PCS, UGC & All University Examinations

Chapterwise Researched
QUESTIONS & ANSWERS
Solved papers & very helpful for your assignments preparation

Hindi & English Medium

  GULLYBABA PUBLISHING HOUSE PVT. LTD.
2525/193, 1st Floor, Onkar Nagar-A, Tri Nagar, Delhi-110035, (From Kanhaiya Nagar Metro Station Towards Old Bus Stand)

Email : hello@gullybaba.com
Web : www.gullybaba.com

Join us on Facebook at /gphbooks

For any Guidance & Assistance Call:
9350849407

Chapter-3

Indian Media Scene

Q1. What do you understand by mass media?
Ans. Mass media is often linked to the word "communication" which generally refers to an exchange of information and messages. Mass media which involves in Newspapers, Radio, Television, Films, and the like, refers to methods of message transmission over space and time. According to historical evidence, oral (word of mouth) exchange of news was the common method of communication in ancient India, whereas the modern medium of communication system was originated since the end of the eighteenth century. The print media, Radio, TV, and Films are taken into account as comprised of Indian mass media. Having understood that the nature of mass media is determined by social conditions, an exceptional attempt is made to understand Indian mass media as a manifestation of social implications in association with the society of India. Indian mass media is a symbol as well as a reflection of India society, which is extremely heterogeneous, diverse, and most importantly, a place of wide range of opinions.

Q2. What is Development and growth of Press (print media), Television, Radio, Cinema, Outdoor media in India?
Ans. The history of organised development communication in India can be traced to rural radio broadcast in the 1940's. Independent India's earliest organised experiments in development communication started with communication development projects initiated by the union government in the 1950's. Different medium was used in the following manner for development purpose:

(1) Newspaper: It is a medium of Development Communication: The power of the press arises from its ability of appearing to the minds of the people and being capable of moving their hearts. However, it has been noticed that the press has not met the requisite interest in developmental communication. In order to correct the imbalances noticed in the media coverage of Rural Development Programs and to ensure that these programs are portrayed in proper perspective, several steps are taken to sensitise the media about issues relating to rural development. The Ministry on a regular basis interacts with the Press mainly through the Press Information Bureau (PIB). Review press conference, press tours and workshops are organised through PIB, with the financial assistance from the Ministry, so as to sensitise press persons about Rural Development Program. For the purpose of creating awareness in respect of rural develop programs among the general public and opinion makers and for disseminating information about new initiatives, the Ministry issues advertisements at regular intervals in national and regional press through DAVP. To enable people in rural areas to access information on Rural Development Program a booklet Gram Vikas' Programs at a glance is brought out in regional languages.

(2) Radio: It is a means of development communication: Radio from its very inception played an important role in development communication; this is mainly due to its advantage of reaching to a large number of people from difference section of the society. Universities and other educational institutes' especially agricultural universities, through their extension networks and international organisations under the UN umbrella carried the development communication experiment. Community radio is another important medium which is growing in importance especially in rural India. Here, NGOs and educational institutions are given license to set up a local community radio station to broadcast information and messages on developmental aspects. Participation of local community is encouraged. As community radio provides a platform to villager to broadcast local issues, it has the potential to get positive action. All India Radio has been the forerunner in the process of implementing communication strategy adopted by the government. The Radio Rural Forum experiment of 1956 covered 156 villages. It contained 30 minute duration program two days a week on different issues like agriculture and varied subjects that could promote rural development. Efforts are being constantly made to use radio for social change. Apart from radio rural forum, other continuous efforts are being made to bring in development. More recently, NGOs have helped broadcast program on women and legal rights etc. On the basis of the Verghese Committee (1978) report which recommended a franchise system for promoting local radio for education and development. Several NGOs use local radio to further their development activities.

(3) **Television:** It is a Medium for Development Communication: TV in India was introduced in 1959, on an experimental basis. It's very inception was with the aim to see what TV could achieve in community development and formal education. From this we can very well understand the importance of television for development communication. Today, after 50 years of Indian television, we see that broadcasters still broadcast program with an eye on social responsibility, serials that incorporate socially relevant themes, interactive talk shows and open forums with government representatives responding to audience queries are popular programs. In 1967, Delhi Television centre launched Krishi Darshan Program at the behest of Dr. Bikram Sarabhai and Prof R. S. Swaminathan. The object of this program was popularisation of modern method in agriculture through the television. TV has been used as an aid to satellite communication technology to effectively bring in development. Satellite communications technology offers unique capability of being able to reach out to very large numbers spread over large distances even in the most remote corners of the country.

(4) **Cinema:** Indian cinema has an identity that is very unique and unmatched. We have moved from the black and white silent films to 3D, but our cinema continues to retain its basic essence - to thrill. Even as internet downloads and television continue to cannibalise the theatrical revenues of Indian films, the lure of the 35 mm is something else altogether. It was Phalke who introduced India to word cinema. Indian cinema turned 100 on April 21, 2012. In a country where over 1,000 films are made every year, in several languages. <u>Bollywood</u> movies, naturally comprise the majority of Indian film industry, while regional films make up the rest (Tamil, Telugu, Kannada, Malayalam, Marathi, Oriya, Bengali, Gujarati, Bhojpuri etc), the Indian movies have just about touched every genre of entertainment.

(5) **Outdoor Media:** Outdoor advertising in India may finally be coming of age. There are several reasons for this. For one, the definition of "outdoor advertising" has undergone a rather dramatic change. "Any advertorial content displayed at any contact point outside the home comes under the purview of this term now", the outdoor medium, in fact, has always had the reach and is also, arguably, among the cheapest vehicles available. The major constraint, though, was quality. The evolution of large

format digital printing solved that problem and now, even high-end marketers, are turning to the outdoor advertisement segment. "The outdoor medium has emerged as a significant alternative to satellite TV channels and the print media". But historically, this segment has been controlled mostly by small-scale and local level hoardings companies and is, therefore, highly fragmented. But over the last year, some consolidation has started in this space. Agencies such as Kinetic (the outdoor media buying arm of the WPP Group) and Prime site (promoted by Mudra) are making significant inroads into this sector. Outdoor advertising is about 17 per cent of the ₹266 billion Indian advertising industry. It is expected to grow at 12 per cent plus for the next few years.

Q3. What is the total expenditure growth of various advertising medium in India?

Ans. The Indian media industry is estimated to grow from INR 646.0 billion in 2010, at a CAGR (compound annual growth rate) of 13.2% for the next five years to reach INR 1198.9 billion in 2015. The television industry is projected to continue to be the major contributor to the overall industry revenue pie and is estimated to grow at a healthy rate of 14.5% cumulatively over the next five years, from an estimated INR 306.5 billion in 2010 to reach INR 602.5 billion by 2015. In the television pie, television distribution is projected to garner a share of 62% in 2015 while television advertising is expected to have 33% share. The television content industry will have a five-per-cent share. Distribution share is expected to hold despite a robust growth in advertisement on the back of the hope that addressable digitisation will cover the entire country by 2015. Of the advertising industry pie, the television advertising industry is projected to command a share of 42.5% in 2015, from a present share of 41.0%. The Indian film industry has had two consecutive bad years in 2009 and 2010 and has shown considerable decline. The industry depends heavily on big films and worthwhile content. With many big films slated to release in the next couple of years, we expect this industry to recover and grow at a CAGR of 9.3% over the next five years, reaching to INR 136.5 billion in 2015 from the present INR 87.5 billion in 2010. However, the growth is subject to the quality of content. 3D films and increasing digital screens are expected to help the film industry garner greater revenue.

Q4. What is the role of NRS & IRS in India?

Ans. Indian Readership Survey or IRS is one of the largest readership survey conducted in India. , IRS covers readership for newspapers, internet usage, and television viewership. Established in 1995 IRS data is widely used by media planners for finalising the media strategy. Besides giving the readership habits, IRS also provides valuable insights into the consumption habits of the Indian consumer. The information covered by IRS are:- Media data study include, Press Readership: 350 + Publications, TV:150+ channels, Cinema, Internet, Radio Listener ship: 15+ Radio Stations, Product data for the following is captured 70+ FMCG products usage and consumption habits,30+ Durable products ownership details Financial Services Urban & Rural Lifestyle Indicators, Telecom Data IRS uses sample from 24 states 91 cities covering a 250,000 respondents. IRS survey results are dissected by the media executives to prove their reach and cost advantages. IRS is done twice a year. IRS is used by most of the media planners. This is a sample based results, one can always question the statistical inferences. Every time the survey results are out, there are bound to be objections and blaming. To counter IRS, another survey is also there in the readership domain i.e. National Readership Survey (NRS). In India is the largest survey of its kind in the world, with a sample sise of over 2,61,212 house-to-house interviews to track the media exposure and changing consumer trends in both urban and rural India - and of course the estimated readership of publications. Combining both the results help media planners to chose the right media across markets. But all these surveys give only approximations. There is no guarantee that a 100 cc ad at the front page of the best daily in India can deliver the desired results. Hence marketers invent a new term: Opportunity to See (OTS). By putting an ad in the front page you are giving the reader an opportunity to see the advertisement how wise

Q5. What is the role of media in rural area?

Ans. Rural Marketing in India Economy has always played an influential role in the lives of people. In India, leaving out a few metropolitan cities, all the districts and industrial townships are connected with rural markets. India has a population that is large, heterogeneous, largely English speaking and a cultural heritage that runs back to thousands of years. The common binding factor being the historical background, over two hundred years of subjugation and the democratic republic it has developed into. Yet the most common factor is the lives of more than seventy percent of its population that lives in the rural areas and has similar economic and social circumstances. The major segmentation of mass population is located in rural area. The market potential is huge in rural areas. Now days even the educational Institutions are concentrating on rural marketing, have developed special management programmers to cater to rural marketing and are doing market research in rural places. Rural markets are rapidly growing in India but have often been ignored by marketers. The statistics of rural markets is: forty six percent of soft drinks are sold in rural markets, forty nine percent of motorcycles and fifty nine percent of cigarettes are also consumed by rural and small town consumers. Apart from this fifty three percent of Fast Moving Consumer Goods and fifty nine percent of consumer durables have market in the rural areas. There are nearly 42,000 rural haats (markets) in India. LIC sells more than 50 percent of its policies in rural India. Of the 20 millions who have signed up for Rediff mail, 60 percent are from small towns The 30 million Kisan Credit Cards (KCC) issued so far exceed the 25 million credit-plus-debit cards issued in urban. These statistics clearly show a trend where the rural consumers are not only buying to fulfill their bare necessities but are also taking care of higher needs of comfort and socialisation. Moreover they have turned highly technology savvy as demonstrated through the success of ITCs echaupals and Rediff's rural success.

Chapter-4

Planning Communication Strategy

Q1. What do you mean by promotion strategy?
Ans. Promotional strategy enables coordination of the different component of the promotion mix that help the organisation to communicate with the consumer. Promotional strategy objectives vary among organisations. Some use promotion to expand their markets, others to hold their current positions, still others to present a corporate viewpoint on a public issue. Promotional strategies can also be used to reach selected markets. Most sources identify the specific promotional objectives or goals of providing information, differentiating the product, increasing sales. The responsibility of developing strategies for each of the component of the promotion mix and formulating an integrated promotion strategy lies with the marketing department of the organisation.

Q2. What are the factors to be considered while farming of the promotional strategy?
Ans. The factor to considered during the making of the promotional strategy are as follows:
(1) Objectives: Your objectives are keys to the success of your communications strategy. Your communications activity is not an end in itself but should serve and hence be aligned with your organisational objectives. Ask yourself what you can do within communications to help your organisation achieve its core objectives. Aligning your communications and organisational objectives will also help to reinforce the importance and relevance of communications and thereby make a

convincing case for the proper resourcing of communications activity within your organisation.

(2) Audiences: You should identify those audiences with whom you need to communicate to achieve your organisational objectives. The best audiences to target in order to achieve an objective may not always be the most obvious ones, and targeting audiences such as the media may not always help achieve your objectives. Everyone would like a higher media and political profile, yet activities aiming towards this may ultimately be self-serving and only communications driven, with no wider impact.

(3) Messages: Strategic targeting and consistency are key to your organisation's messages. Create a comprehensive case covering all the key messages, and emphasise the different elements of the case for different audiences. To maximise impact you should summaries the case in three key points which can be constantly repeated. Remember that communications is all about storytelling: use interesting narrative, human interest stories and arresting imagery.

(4) Tools and activities: Identify the tools and activities that are most appropriate to communicating the key messages to the audiences. These will be suggested by your audiences, messages, or a combination of the two. For example, an annual report is a useful tool in corporate communications whereas an email newsletter lends itself well to internal communications. Ensure that you tailor your tools and activities to the level of time and human and financial resources available.

(5) Resources and timescales: The key rules to observe are always to deliver what you promise and never over promise. Use your resources and timescales to set legitimate levels of expectations and outline the case for more dedicated resources.

(6) Evaluation and amendment: Consider performing a communications audit to assess the effectiveness of your strategy with both your internal and external audiences. You should use open questions with appropriate prompts and benchmarks and, if possible, get someone independent to do the work. Consider and discuss the results carefully and use them to amend your strategy.

Example audiences to consider are your staff, funders, key political targets and media. Questions you should consider asking are:
- What do you read/see/hear?
- What works/doesn't work?
- What do you want to see more of?
- What information do you need that you are not currently supplied with?

- How often do you want us to communicate with you?

Q3. Explain decision sequence analysis for promotional planning.

Ans. Following figure illustrates a decision sequence analysis for promotional strategy. It provides an illustration of the stages in the promotional planning framework discussed in the previous section. It should be noted that the decision sequence analysis is:

- based on an 'adaptive' process. It, thus, includes systematic procedures for gathering information and bringing about modification when needed in the promotional planning.
- based on the proposition that the promotional planning is a continual and ongoing process. Evaluation, feedback and follow up are the integral parts of the process that provide it with vitality and relevance in the changing needs of promotion.

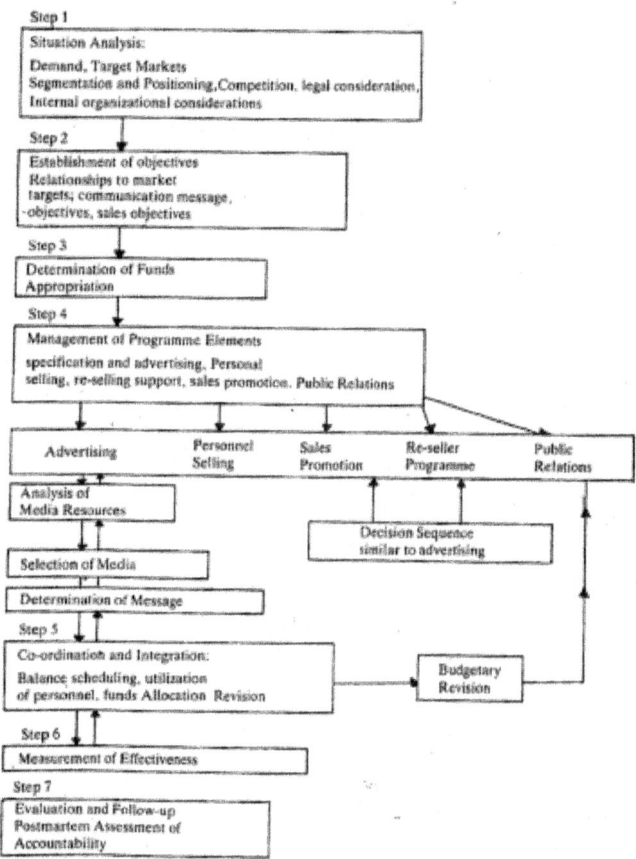

Fig. 4.1: Decision Sequence Analysis of Promotional Strategy

❑❑❑

WE'D LOVE IT IF YOU'D LIKE US!

/gphbooks

We're now on Facebook!

Like our page to stay on top of the useful, greatest headlines & exciting rewards.

Our other awesome Social Handles:

gphbooks
For awesome &
informative videos
for IGNOU students

9350849407
Order now
through WhatsApp

gphbooks
We are
in pictures

gphbook
Words you get
empowered by

Chapter-5

Advertising Campaign Planning-Strategic Consideration, Creative Consideration

Q1. How message design can help in positioning?

Ans. Positioning covers a broad category of marketing activities that are designed to shape out your target markets and define your approach to those markets. It includes such issues as: Market segmentation, Competitive positioning, Market sizing and analysis, Product marketing and Core messaging. A complete positioning project/document should address all of these elements and more. Issues like pricing, potential partners, and distribution strategy should also be considered. The key is to remember that when you are talking about positioning, it is the big stuff, not the small stuff. Essentially, positioning encompasses all of those factors that determine where and how your company's products and services "fit" in a given market.

Messaging is the final strategic step before entering the execution stage of marketing. Messaging is the art of defining what you will say to the markets you are targeting. I used the word "core" messaging here because there are different levels of messaging. Core messaging helps you nail down the major points that you want to make when you are talking to a key market or audience. Core messaging serves as the foundation for all the execution programs; more tailored messages are developed subsequently to appeal to the specific audience you are reaching. It is highly recommended that you test your core messages with friendly customers or analysts before you begin to use them in marketing campaigns, programs, or events. The cost of testing them is much cheaper than finding out they don't work after you've made a major investment in a marketing campaign. Once you begin to execute, you'll be entering the "rubber meets the road" phase; if there are defects in your strategy or message, you'll soon find out, and then you'll have sunk costs to deal with. You want to insure the credibility of your message before you begin program execution. There's no way around it. Your market changes, your competitors change, your channel changes. As a result, messaging must constantly be refined and improved. As you become smarter about the buying behavior in your target markets, you can create stronger, more focused messages that have impact

Q2. How message can be present effectively by using one or two-sided message?

Ans. Messages can be presented in two ways: Central and Peripheral. A well documented-ad, giving rational advantages and disadvantages of the product initiates active cognitive information processing (Central, presentation). Research has shown that messages that are consistent with the self images of respondents tend to take the Central route. Information relating to quantitative aspects generally relies on peripheral like the spokesperson to affect interest. Some marketers distinguish between rational and emotional appeal presentations. The distinction in the two approaches can be seen in ads that make heavy use of emotional, symbolic cues as against straightforward presentation. Researchers argue that it is impossible to design a completely rational or a completely emotional message.

If the audience initially favors' the communicator's position, or if it is not likely to hear an opposing argument, then a one-sided (supportive) communication that stresses only favorable information is most effective. However, if the audience is critical or friendly, if it is well educated, or if it is likely to hear opposing claims, then a two-sided (reputational) message is most effective. Some recent research suggests that claim credibility can be enhanced by actually disclaiming superiority in some product features in relation to a competing brand. Communication researchers not only have explored the problem of persuading audiences to take some prescribed action (e.g. to buy a product), but also have investigated ways to keep existing customers safe from outside persuasion. Their findings suggest that two-sided appeals containing both pro and con arguments about the brand serve to inculcate consumers against arguments that may be raised by competitors. In effect, this strategy provides consumers with counter-arguments with which to rationalise against future attacks by competing brands. A practical illustration of two-side advertising is seen in comparative advertising, a marketing strategy used by increasing numbers of marketers. Although comparative advertising is widely used, it is not without critics.

Researchers dispute its effectiveness in aiding message recall. Some maintain the message-recall effectiveness of comparative ads is somewhat higher than that of ads which do not explicitly name the competition.

Q3. What are the important elements of print advertising?

Ans. Print advertising includes sales brochures, coupons, fliers, business cards, billboards and ads in magazines and newspapers. Use this medium successfully by first defining the advertising goal, identifying your target audience and focusing your message. The cost of printed advertising can easily outweigh its benefit, so never waste it. Each of the seven elements of print advertising must enhance your ad's effectiveness.

- **Text:** The text must communicate in clear, concise and focused language. Start with a headline that grabs the reader's attention, sparks interest in your product and conveys your message succinctly. Potential customers have only seconds to read your billboard. Even in brochures or catalogs, keep body copy brief and on point. Include the company signature --- your identifying slogan and/or logo. Use fonts (typefaces) that complement your message and are easy to read.

- **Graphic Elements:** Photography, illustration and logo symbols like Nike's swoosh raise interest in any ad. Integrate these graphic elements with your headline and copy for maximum effect. A study by Texas State University showed that more attention goes to pictures than words and human models get the most attention in magazine ads. This indicates the value of using models that match or appeal to your target audience to forge an immediate connection between your product/service and your potential customer. Inconsistency between your headline and your illustration will confuse the viewer and reduce the ad's impact.

- **Color vs. B&W:** Color printing costs more than black and white. Full-color printing uses four inks and four runs through the press for each page. Two-color printing is a cheaper color option, appropriate for some applications.

- **Layout:** The layout is the way you put all the elements together to create the final ad. Your layout needs a focal point --- usually the picture or headline --- for readers' eyes to land on, then the white space, graphic and text elements should lead them through the copy to the company signature. Make the final layout match the ad's ultimate printed appearance in every detail.

- **Sise and Shape:** Newspaper and magazine placement fees are based on ad sise. The exact dimensions may vary by publication, but are priced as fractions of a page. Special locations, like the back cover, cost more. Use appropriate sise and shape, linked to purpose and corporate image, for non-publication print advertising.

- **Paper and Ink:** For print ads other than in magazines or newspapers, choose paper with a composition, weight and finish that contributes positively to your advertising image. Traditional inks contain volatile organic compounds; consider using soy-based inks if they will give the result you want.

- **Placement:** Placement of your print advertising affects its success. An auto parts dealer will get more response running his ad in an automotive magazine or classified section than in a fashion magazine. Direct mail solicitations generate leads more effectively than magazine ads do.

- **Header:** The header, also known as the title, attracts attention to the ad and lets the reader know what he will find out in the copy. The header should communicate a key benefit described in the ad, such as a discount sale or a limited-time offer. It may also identify a problem a reader might have and propose a solution to the problem. The header is commonly the strongest element of a print advertisement, and can determine whether the viewer reads the remainder of the ad.

- **Image:** An image at the top or in the body of the ad creates curiosity and communicates what the viewer will learn by continuing to read the ad Newspaper advertisements are typically black-and-white, but a color image can increase the impact of the ad Choose an image relevant to the product or service for sale, and use one, strong image if possible to keep the ad simple.

- **Body:** Print advertisements commonly include a body, which is the main part of the ad the body elaborates on the concept of the title, and should build interest in the product or service. Print ad copy should be well organised. Use bullet points or sub headers when appropriate to make the information easily understandable for the reader.

- **Call to Action:** A call to action typically follows the ad copy. As the name suggests, a call to action leads the reader to take a specific action, such as visiting the store or contacting the store for more information. Because readers can quickly forget the body copy, the call to action needs to create a sense of urgency. Phrases like "call today" and "this offer expires ..." with a date direct the reader to do something now.

- **Contact Information:** Contact information tells the viewer how to get in touch with the business to take advantage of the offer. Include as much information as appropriate to make it easy for the reader to find the business. This section usually includes the company name, address, telephone number and website address.

Q4. Briefly describe message design and marketing objectives.

Ans. The message is the though idea, attitude, image or other information that the sender wishes to convey to the intended audience.

The marketer's objectives tend to vary with audience. Objectives in communicating with consumers, for example, may be one or all of the following: (1) informing them what is for sale, (2) creating brand awareness, (3) getting them to buy the product, (4) reducing their uneasiness after the purchase is made. The marketer's objective with intermediary customers is to get them to stock the product; with other manufacturers, to get them to buy the product and use it to make their own.

Senders must also know their audiences' characteristics in terms of education, interests, needs, and realms of experience. They must then endeavour to encode or phrase their message in such a way that they will fall within the consumers' zones of understanding and familiarity.

To attract the attention and interest of their target audiences, marketers start their advertisements with an appeal to the needs and interests of the audience, and end with an appeal relevant to their own needs (with an effective sales closing). Advertisements that do not conclude with an 'action' closing tend to provoke much less action on the part of the consumer than those that do. Table 1 lists twelve techniques summarised to make messages more memorable and persuasive.

Table 5.1: Communication techniques that make messages memorable

(1) Get the audience aroused.
(2) Give the audience a reason for listening.
(3) Use questions to generate involvement.
(4) Cast the message in terms familiar to your audience and build on points of interest.
(5) Use thematic organisation - the material together by a theme and present in a logical, irreversible sequence.
(6) Use subordinate category words; i.e. more concrete, specific terms, (Example: duck rather than bird, duck being a subordinate word to bird).
(7) Repeat key points.
(8) Use rhythm and rhyme.
(9) Use concrete rather than abstract terms.
(10) Use the Zeigamik effect-leave the audience with an incomplete message, something to ponder so that they have to make an effort to achieve closure.
(11) Ask your audience for a conclusion.
(12) Tell the audience the implications of their conclusion.

Q5. What do you mean by message presentation.

Ans. Messages can be presented in two ways - Central and Peripheral. The former use the direct and central route to persuasion. A well documented-ad, giving rational advantages and disadvantages of the product initiates active cognitive information processing (Central ,presentation). An example could be the ad for Voltas refrigerator talking rationally of various product features in the ad format.

Peripheral message was for example scenic backgrounds on title music on the other hand provide pleasant association, aid recall and provoke favourable inferences about product advantages.

Research has shown that messages that are consistent with the self images of respondents tend to take the Central route. Information relating to quantitative aspects generally rely on peripheral like the spokesperson to affect interest.

Some marketers distinguish between rational and emotional appeal presentations. The distinction in the two approaches can be seen in ads that make heavy use of emotional, symbolic cues as against straightforward presentation. An example would be the message for ceasefire fire extinguisher. On the other hand researchers argue that it is impossible to design a completely rational or a completely emotional message.

Q6. What do you mean by message development. Briefly describe its tools.

Ans. Television, Radio, Print, Hoardings, Direct Mail. These are just a few channels, among countless others, through which, a marketer communicates his ideas to his prospect, the consumer.

And what is the result of the proliferation of a variety of products and an ever growing number of marketers? A lot of communication, In all directions. From all Directions. Direct. Indirect. Zigzag. All.

Also over communication? Yes

So what's the problem?

To be noticed. To be seen and heard in the crowd. In addition to the difficult task of persuading the consumer to act favourably.

Like any other mode of communication an effective ad too emerges from a powerful idea. The idea need not be only strong but it should also be unique. Capable of standing out in the crowd.

Translating the idea comes next. Into a language to which the consumer is likely to respond best. And this requires a lot of creativity. The success of the idea depends on this translation. On creativity.

Creativity is the quality of being able to produce original work or ideas by human intelligence and imagination in any field.

We have come to an important juncture now. Can originality be described and explained in the limited few pages that follow? Of course not.

A new creation can win praise of people only if it is completely new. Something that 'had never existed before.

But would you not call a man at sea also creative who improvises a raft from driftwood. He devices something from what is at hand. The idea of a raft is not new, but preparing one from available material does call for a lot of creativity.

Naturally, our study touches upon originality and improvisation, both.

For creating a good ad there are a few tools that are normally used. These are like chisel and mallet, for transforming ideas into meaningful shapes. These are the means towards achieving the goal.

Important elements in print advertising are:

(1) Sise and Shapes (2) Headline (3) Illustration (4) Body Copy (5) Colours and (6) Composition.

These elements are used to design and develop the message in a way that the basic objective of communication is fulfilled. Be it informing the consumer about the sale, or persuading him to buy the merchandise or simply creating an awareness about the brand

❏❏❏

Chapter-6

Advertising Creativity Campaign Planning and Execution

Q1. What is creativity all about in advertising?

Ans. Creativity is a very subjective term. There are different opinions for this term, on what we individually think is creative. Some people believe creativity is an engrained concept that you are born with it. Other people believe it is a talent that can be learned and taught. The essential elements of creativity are really imagination and inventiveness disciplined by routine skills. Your imagination is something you are born with, it can be large and wild or it can be small and constrained. Inventiveness is something that can be disciplined; it can be taught and learned with practice and skill. Put these two concepts together and anything is possible.

In advertising, agencies live and die by creative communications. Creativity is one of the reasons clients justify advertising and their choice of agencies. So in advertising creativity is exactly, some creative commercials are effective, some effective ads are creative, and other ads are neither creative nor effective. Creativity and effectiveness ultimately join in the consumer's minds rather than remain separate. Now what is efficiency, efficiency is a effectiveness of an ad which is determined by the correct combination of its impact and retention. Impact is the ability of an ad to attract attention and retention being the ability of an ad to stay on viewers' minds. We can thus say with certainty that an advertisement needs to be creative to succeed. Its creativity needs to be effective in both its impact and retention. Although creativity in advertising is an important factor, one must remember to not be creative just for creative sake. The creativity must also be effective. Successful creative strategies result from pinpointing an idea, a nuance, an insight, or a nugget of information gleaned from research or sometime from an intuitive understanding or quickness of human nature. The true role of the strategy is to make that intuitive leap which defines the relationship between the brand and its user.

Q2. How celebrity can help in advertising?

Ans. There are a number of advantages to using celebrities in advertising, whether you are running print, Internet, radio or television commercials. The key for small companies is making sure the local celebrity is relevant and has broad appeal. Popular celebrities often work best because they naturally generate lots of attention. Celebrities are most effective if they promote products or services they are most likely to use. In other words, they must be plausible consumers, such as a local newscaster wearing a business suit from an area men's store.

- **Influence Consumer Purchases:** The affinity consumers have for certain celebrities can greatly influence their purchases. People may have the attitude, "If the product is good enough for her, its good enough for me." This philosophy is often the impetus behind advertisements for makeup, skin creams, hair products and attire. Consumers may also desire the same soft drink as their team's best baseball player.

- **Build Awareness:** Celebrities in advertising build brand awareness, according to "Supermarket News," a publication covering the food distribution industry. And they build it much more quickly than traditional types of advertising. Brand awareness measures the percentage of people who are familiar with a particular brand. Small businesses spend lots of money and time for exposure to incrementally increase brand awareness among consumers.

- **Position a Brand:** Some small companies use celebrities in advertising to position their brands. Product positioning is placing a company's products in the best possible light in the minds of a target group.

- **Attract New Users:** One challenge small company's face is finding new users for their products. Celebrities in advertising appeal to customers as well as those who have never tried the brand. The latter may be users of competitive brands. However,

those who continually see the celebrity in a commercial for a certain product may be convinced to try the product.
- **Breathe Life Into Failing Brand:** The use of a celebrity in an advertisement may also help to breathe life into a failing brand. For example, a small soap manufacturer might think about dropping a brand or product, especially if production and overhead costs are leaving little or no profit. However, the use of a celebrity to tout the benefits of the brand could help create new interest and excitement in consumers.

Q3. What association is between creativity and advertisement?

Ans. Some of the creative association in the advertisement is defined as:

(1) Unique Selling Proposition: The basic idea of creative advertising being unique for selling a product has been coined by different authorities in different ways. There are three guidelines to the development of an USP. First, the proposition needs to involve a specific benefit. Second, it must be **unique**, one that competing firms are not using. Third, it must sell. Therefore, it must be important enough to the consumer to influence the decision process.

(2) Brand Image: Advertisement should be thought of as a contribution of the complex symbol which is the brand image. Most manufacturers do not accept any limitation on the image of their brands. They want it be all things to all people. Those who find expedient to change image of their brand want it change upward. Often it has acquired a bargain basement image, a useful asset in times of economic scarcity, but a grave embarrassment in boom days, when the majority of consumers are on the way of social ladder. He asserted that "build sharply defined personalities for their brand and stick to those personalities year after year. It is the total personality of the brand rather than any trivial product difference which decides its ultimate position in the market.

(3) Reality: The present creative idea has changed its perspective to be more nearer to truth and creative person are applying an idea which looks, feels and speaks like reality.

(4) Comparison: The comparative advertisement may be defined as an advertisement consist of three basic features:
- Two or more specifically named' or recognizably demand and rated brands of the product or service category are compared.

- The campaign based on one or more attributes of the goods or services.
- It is either stated implied or demonstrated that factual information has been gathered as a basis for the comparative claims.

(5) Jingle: Jingle may be defined as an advertising message, usually in verse form, sung to musical -accompaniment. A jingle is used in television/radio as part of a commercial to express a theme or product story.

(6) Slogans: Slogan may be considered as a basic idea of a product symbolising its creativity and ensure the success of a campaign. It provides continuity for the campaign crystallises in a few memorable words. The key ideas are theme one wants to associate with a product.

(7) Headline: Headline is an essential and important element of the advertisement. Its newness, advice, promise, curiosity generating approach, selectivity and commanding characteristic play important role for creative advertisement. The basic features of headlines are its attractiveness, generating among consumers and creative. Prospective for the selective of right prospects, the primary job of any headline is to attract the attention of the potential customers. Virtually headlines are a phrase of words that have innate ability to flag reader attentions.

(8) Relevance: Creative ideas consist of relevance and newness. Relevance means the theme of an ad must be targeted for audience with positive importance and creative involvement.

(9) Emotion: In the field of advertising emotion or mood creation approach requires a basic strategic plan. Mood creation ads are particularly useful for products or services that lack distinctions characteristics. Emotional appeal generates feelings which further work as energies that sell products. Emotion like surprise, gratitude, acceptance, expectancy, happiness, relief and excitement create satisfaction or dissatisfaction and therefore, its use should be ensured in a creative way.

(10) Positioning: Is a strategic tool of a brand managers and advertising planners. The position of a brand is a perception which brings about in the mind of target consumers. This perception reflects the essence of brand in terms of its functional and non-functional benefit in the judgment of the consumer. It is relative to the perception held by that consumer of competing brand, all which can be represented as points or position his or her perceptual space and all together, make up product class.

(11) Benefit: Benefit in the creative advertising means attributes of the product presented before targeted customers with planned strategic way. Because consumer always buy product 'test, texture, nutritional value as ability to clean or brighten, in other words they buy a product benefit.

(12) Negative: Negative advertising is also a trend generated by demand of creativity. Such advertisements show the dark uninviting side of thing like homeliness, sadness, etc. Though in the world of advertisement such idea has been generated to repulse the consumer into remembering but it has been not found in good taste.

(13) Celebrity: Numerous advertising campaigns used personalities generally from the motion picture industry, sports world and theater. However, personalities can also be average individuals. Celebrities are those people who are widely known. When such people appear in advertisement they do so as presenters and spokesperson. A presenter may provide a testimonial about the excellence of the product whereas spokesperson does not endorse the product rather the personality speaks further about the company. The process of selecting celebrity as a personality of an ad campaign requires number of criteria. A product that is designed to project an image may find that image can be enhanced by a particular type of celebrity. It means that compatibility ensure along with-acceptance of the individual by the target audience. These ads help in increasing the brand recall rating among consumer significantly.

(14) Execution: Execution is the ultimate goal of advertisement which is to determine the real communication of a persuasive message to the audience. There are certain characteristics of execution, Audience respectability, honesty of advertisement, simple clean and direct approach are some of the basic characteristic which ensure creative execution. It should stand out from others.

(15) Humor: Humor enhances attention of audience. It is used to advertising to attract attention and direct attention to the product in a pointed and involving way. Humor not only entertains people but disarm them as well - it makes people drop their good. It can work at the start and at the end of an ad

Q4. How execution plays an important role in creative advertising?

Ans. Creative execution refers to the manner in which an advertising appeal is carried out or presented. A particular advertising appeal can be executed in a variety of ways and a particular means of execution can be applied to a variety of advertising appeals. Some of the more commonly used execution techniques include:

(1) Straight-sell or factual message: This type of execution relies on a straightforward presentation of information about the product or service such as specific attributes or benefits.

(2) Scientific/technical evidence: A variation of the straight sells where scientific or technical evidence or information is presented in the ad to support a claim.

(3) Demonstration: This type of execution is designed to illustrate the key advantages or benefits of a product or service by showing it in actual use or in some contrived or staged situation.

(4) Comparison: This type of execution involves a direct or indirect comparison of a brand against the competition.

(5) Testimonials: Many advertisers present their advertising messages in the form of a testimonial whereby a person speak on behalf of the product or service based on his or her personal use of and/or experiences with it.

(6) Slice of life: This type of execution is often based on a problem/solution type of format. The ad attempts to portray a real-life situation involving a problem, conflict or situation consumers may face in their daily lives. The ad then focuses on showing how the advertiser's product or service can resolve the problem. Slice-of-life executions are also becoming very common in business-to-business advertising as companies use this approach to demonstrate how their products and services can be used to solve business problems.

(7) Animation: This technique used animated characters or scenes drawn by artists or on computer. Animation is often used as an execution technique for advertising targeted at children.

(8) Personality Symbol: This type of execution involves the use of a central character or personality symbol to deliver the advertising message and with which the product or service can be identified. The personality symbol can take the form of a person who is used as a spokesperson, animated characters or even animals.

(9) Fantasy: This type of appeal is often used for image advertising by showing an imaginary situation or illusion involving a consumer and the product or service. Cosmetic companies often use fantasy executions although the technique has also been used in advertising.

(10) Dramatisation: This execution technique creates a suspenseful situation or scenario in the form of a short story. Dramatisations often use the problem/solution approach as they show how the advertised brand can help resolve a problem.

(11) Humor: Humor can be used as the basis for an advertising appeal. However, humor can also be used as a way of executing the message and presenting other types of advertising appeals.

(12) Combinations: Many of these execution techniques can be combined in presenting an advertising message. For example, slice-of-life ads are often used to demonstrate a product or make brand comparisons

Q5. Briefly describe creative process.

Ans. The creative process has been described, using a variety of models, suggesting that, "the process was a matter of stages, the creative individual paves through in a quest to solve problem identified, preparation incubation, illumination and verification. The preparation stage includes the orientation of an individual towards a problem and the gathering of informations needed to help to solve that problem. The second stage of incubation includes the period prior to the discovery of an idea or problem solution. The third stage identified illumination, is the emergence of idea or solution and the last one is actual working of an idea. In this way one can ascertain that process of creativity is a system consisting of gradual stages with which an individual can solve the ultimate problem.

Theories of the creative process are based on the steps in the creative process. Orientation, preparation analysis, hypothesis,. incubation, synthesis and verification are some of the phases which have been undertaken by the most of the proponents of the theory of creative process. All these theories have something in common and particularly highlighting the track of ideas in which assessment of the situation is the primary stage. Thereafter, the individual involves in creation defined the problem and use the subconscious ideas followed by rationalising the ideas and judging the best one to create a solution were primary objects of creative process. The art of creation takes place within this process. The advertisement consisting of scientific aid more rational creative process could be more effective than a non-creative by-product. In this connection it is pointed out that the creative people plays a basic role and he is the agent of creative process.

◻◻◻

Feedback is the breakfast of Champions.

Ken Blanchard

You can Help other students.
"Inform any error or mistake in this book."

We and Universe
will reward you for Your Kind act.

Email at : feedback@gullybaba.com
or
WhatsApp on 9350849407

Chapter-7

Advertising Research - Role and Trends

Q1. Discuss the tools and techniques of major types of advertising research.

Ans. Advertising research covers several of research done for evaluation of advertising campaigns. These ranges from copy test to strategy tests to brand personality to media research, which are as follows:-

- **Recall Measurement:** Recall is normally used to determine to what extent advertising messages have been retained by consumers. The assumption is made that recall of an advertising message and purchase behavior are somewhat related. Thus, recall is believed to be an important measure for the advertising campaign. It can be measured by aided or unaided:

  Unaided recall: In this method the respondent is given no clue as to what brand is being investigated or what additional questions might be asked. He or she must recall any or all advertising messages seen in the past and relate them to the question. The assumption is made that advertising remembered without any clue from the interviewer is stronger than that remembered with some direction.

  Aided recall: In this method the respondent's reply is aided by the brand name. Rather than trying to remember all flour advertising, the respondent can concentrate on the particular brand. Care must be taken that not too much aid is given or the respondent may resort to guessing rather than recalling.

  The major advantage of measuring recall is that it allows measurement of at least one aspect of the advertising campaign.

If the respondent remembers the campaign message or portions of the actual advertising, a direct correlation can be made. The main problem is that recall and purchase behavior may not be directly connected. In other words, the person may recall the message, but that message may not influence the purchase decision. In addition, because over the year many campaigns appear quite similar, the respondent may actually recall a previous advertising message and put it into the context of the present campaign. It is often difficult to identify or isolate specific campaign features.

- **Attitude Measurement:** Attitude tests are used to measure changes in consumer perceptions of a brand, or degree of acceptance of various claims made in the advertising. Five basic techniques are used to measure attitudes:

  Direct questions: In this technique only closed ended questions are given to the customer. Customer can not give any description related to the product only he/she can about is good or bad in one word. The level or degree of feeling is not possible. As a result, this approach may be combined with a rating scale.

  Rating scale: In this technique rating is done on the basics of excellent, very good, good, average, or bad. Although scales are easy to apply and tabulate, the main problem is correlating the views of the respondents. A product is very good , answer by one person may be the same as an excellent from another. A rating scale does not discriminate sufficiently to permit a precise line to be drawn between the various attitudes.

  Checklists: In this technique also close ended question are given. The attributes can be easily ranked by the respondents and easily tabulated by the advertiser. The primary problem, however, is that there is no assurance that most important factors have been isolated and listed on the questionnaire. In addition, the meaning of each question is not always totally clear. For example, does "Reputation of manufacturer" mean the same thing to all respondents?

  Semantic differential tests: Paired opposite descriptive words or phrases are separated on a scale. The respondent is allowed to check the place on the scale where the product would be rated. Thus, the respondent's attitude towards the product can be determined. The scale is easy to use and the results are simple to tabulate. The major problem with this type of measure is that the scale may not be interpreted by all respondents in the same manner.

Partially structured interviews: In this approach, an attempt is made to allow the respondent to discuss the general topics area and reveal attitudes about the brand without using a specific set of questions. Although the interviewer knows the general areas about information and attitudes will be sought, the use of the unstructured interview allows the respondent an opportunity to indicate areas of interest that might not have been previously considered.

Attitudinal tests are viewed as an important element in advertising campaign evaluation. A favorable attitude is considered to be an indication that the person is more likely to purchase a brand than if he or she has unfavorable attitude. As a result, the changes in attitudes are regarded as more important in advertising evaluation than awareness or recall. Unfortunately, there is little evidence that a favorable attitude will always result in behavioral change, such as purchase of a brand. The use of attitude measurements is also open to question because it is very difficult to obtain an accurate measure of people's attitude about any subject.

- **Brand Usage:** Brand usage is the ultimate measure of the effectiveness of an advertising campaign. Although it has been stressed that, for the most part, advertising should be considered only on the basis of communication efforts, in some instances, advertisers want to trace sales results. This is done by measuring such things as movement of goods through store audits, pantry audits, and consumer panels. When consumer interviews are used, they consist primarily of a series of questions about past, present and future brand usage. By using such type of consumer questionnaire, primarily on a pretest post test basis, changes in purchasing habits can be measured. When these usage changes are combined with tests of awareness, recall and attitudes, determination of the effects of an advertising campaign is sometimes possible. The attempt to relate advertising to sales is sometimes fruitful when all variables can be controlled, although the relationship is somewhat tenuous.

- **Pre-testing**: Also known as copy testing, it is a form of customised research that predicts in-market performance of an ad, before it airs, by analysing audience levels of attention, brand linkage, motivation, entertainment, and communication, as well as breaking down the ad's Flow of Attention and Flow of Emotion. Pre-testing is also used to identify weak spots within an ad to improve performance, to more effectively edit 60's to 30's or 30's to 15's, to select images from the spot to use in an integrated campaign's print ad, to pull out the key moments for use in ad tracking, and to identify branding moments.

  Techniques used in this are given below:

  Qualitative Research: Focus groups research is widely used at the front end of the development of an advertising campaign.

  Audience Impressions of the ad: Many copy tests add a set of open-ended questions to the procedures designed to tap the audience's impressions of what the ad was about, what ideas were presented, interest in the ideas, and so on.

  Adjective checklists: This uses a checklist questionnaire which includes adjectives that allow advertiser to determine how warm, amusing, irritated or informative the respondent it to be.

  Physiological measures: Several kinds of instruments are used to observe reactions to advertisements. In general, they attempt to capture the changes in nervous system or emotional arousal during exposure sequence. Gadgets used primarily consist of eye camera etc.

- **Post-testing**: Tracking studies can be customised or syndicated. Tracking studies provide either periodic or continuous in-market research monitoring a brand's performance, including brand awareness, brand preference, product usage and attitudes. Advertising tracking can be done by telephone interviews or online interviews—with the two approaches producing fundamentally different measures of consumer memories of advertising, recall versus recognition.

- **Media and Custom research:**

  Television Rating Points (TVRs): This research is used in measurement of television audience. In India, as of now, two companies do this kind of research. The viewership measurement is specific to the time bands. Usefulness of this research is that it helps in formulation of media plans. Advertising campaigns can benefit from perfect targeting by using this research.

Press Readership: Comparable of Television Rating Points is readership survey (IRS 1998). This reassert is used in measurement of readership of various print vehicles. Again, like TVRs this research helps in perfect targeting. This research is used primarily while doing, media planning for a campaign. As far as custom research are concerned there are many existing today in the market. Various research companies have developed their own models and offer to do research for advertisers on the basis of their models.

Starch Tests: This is a form of media research done to find out the impact of placing (position) of the advertisements on different pages of a publication. Starch measures three degree of readership:

Noted: The percentage who remember having previously seen the advertisement in the issue or a publication;

Associated: The percentage who saw any part of the ad that clearly indicates the brand or advertiser; and

Read Most: The percentage who read 50% or more of the written material in the advertisement.

Q2. What are the methods of measuring awareness.

Ans. Awareness is generally regarded as a measure of knowledge without reference to source. Although the primary interest in advertising evaluation is knowing if there is a relationship between the advertising and consumer awareness, establishing this relationship is not usually possible. There are four primary methods of measuring awareness;

- **Yes-or-no questions. Example:** "Have you ever heard of Annapurna Atta (flour)?" Yes No Although the yes-no questions are simple to administer and tabulate, no information is gained beyond the direct answer.
- **Open-end questions. Example:** "What companies you can name that package flour?" In this instance, more information is obtained than in yes/no situation, but no relationship to the advertising campaign can be inferred.

- **Check list questions. Example:** "Which of the following products does Kissan Company manufacture?" Flour Ketchup Ginger Sauce. Here the answers are easily obtained, although the range of answers is restricted. As in open-end and yes-no questions, no connection with the advertising campaign can be developed.
- **Rating scales. Example:** "How would you rate Kissan's Flour in comparison with other brands of flours you have used?" Better, About the same as Not as good as With this approach, a measure of familiarity is achieved, but differences among the person doing the rating make it difficult to combine answers or interpret the exact results. Additional scales or other approaches are sometimes used to make this form of measurement more reliable.
- Measurement of awareness through these techniques is quick and fairly low cost because it can be done through the mail or by telephone interview. The results are easy to tabulate and generally straight forward. These advantages are balanced by the lack of knowledge of a significant change in awareness; that is, awareness may have been higher before the campaign than after. Another disadvantage of this is, it is difficult to determine the source of awareness. Awareness may or may not have come from the advertising campaign.

Q3. What basic techniques are used to measure attitudes?

Ans. Recall and attitude tests are often combined in an attempt to determine if there are major differences between consumers who remember the advertising message and those who don't. Attitude tests are also used to measure changes in consumer perceptions of a brand, or degree of acceptance of various claims made in the advertising.

Five basic techniques are used to measure attitudes:
- **Direct questions.** Example: "How would you describe the use of Kissan's Flour for baking?" Only a favourable or unfavourable attitude toward the product is measured. The level or degree of feeling is not possible. As a result, this approach may be combined with a rating scale.
- **Rating scale.** Example: "How would you describe the self-measuring spout on Kissan's Flour packages?" Very easy to uses, Easy to use, Neither easy nor hard to use, Hard to s a y, Very hard to use. Although scales are easy to apply and tabulate, the main problem is correlating the views of the respondents. A

"Very easy to use" answer by one person may be the same as an "Easy to use" response from another. A rating scale does not discriminate sufficiently to permit a precise line to be drawn between the various attitudes.

- **Checklists,** Example: "Which one of the following is most important to you when you purchase flour?" Price , Package , Ease of availability , Reputation of manufacturer . The attributes can be easily ranked by the respondents and easily tabulated by the advertiser. The primary problem, however, is that there is no assurance that most important factors have been isolated and listed on the questionnaire. In addition, the meaning of each question is not always totally clear. For example, does "Reputation of manufacturer" mean the same thing to all respondents?

- **Semantic differential tests.** Example: 'Would you say the user of Kissan's Flour is:

    A good cook____ ____ ____ ____A poor cook

    Extravagant____ ____ ____ ____Price conscious

    Paired opposite descriptive words or phrases are separated on a scale. The respondent is allowed to check the place on the scale where the product would be rated. Thus, the respondent's attitude towards the product can be determined. The scale is easy to use and the results are simple to tabulate. The major problem with this type of measure is that the scale may not be interpreted by all respondents in the same manner.

- **Partially structured interviews.** Example. "I would like you to tell me some of your feelings about baking and the ingredients you use, such as flour, butter and eggs." In this approach, an attempt is made to allow the respondent to discuss the general topics area and reveal attitudes about the brand without using a specific set of questions. Although the interviewer knows the general areas about information and attitudes will be sought, the use of the unstructured interview allows the respondent an opportunity to indicate areas of interest that might not have been previously considered.

Attitudinal tests are viewed as an important element in advertising campaign evaluation. A favourable attitude is considered to be an indication that the person is more likely to purchase a brand than if he or she has unfavourable attitude. As a result, the changes in attitudes are regarded as more important in advertising evaluation than awareness or recall. Unfortunately, there is little evidence that a favourable attitude will always result in behavioural change, such as purchase of a brand. The use of attitude measurements is also open to question because it is very difficult to obtain an accurate measure of people's attitude about any subject.

Q4. What is the pattern of measuring brand usage.

Ans. Brand usage is the ultimate measure of the effectiveness of an advertising campaign. Although it has been stressed that, for the most part, advertising should be considered only on the basis of communication efforts, in some instances, advertisers want to trace sales results. This is done by measuring such things as movement of goods through store audits, pantry audits, and consumer panels. When consumer interviews are used, they consist primarily of a series of questions about past, present and future brand usage For example:

- "What brand of flour do you normally purchase?"

    Kissan' s _____ Pillsbury _____ Kohinoor_____

- "What brand of flour did you buy last?"

    Kissan's _____ Pillsbury _____ Kohinoor_____

- ;'What brand of flour do you think you will buy next?"

    Kissan's_____ Pillsbury _____ Kohinoor_____

By using this type of consumer questionnaire, primarily on a pretest post test basis, changes in purchasing habits can be measured. When these usage changes are combined with tests of awareness, recall and attitudes, determination of the effects of an advertising campaign is sometimes possible. The attempt to relate advertising to sales is sometimes fruitful when all variables can be controlled, although the relationship is somewhat tenuous. (Note that actual purchase behaviour can be observed through in-store scanner data. However, as in the survey methodology, changes in purchase patterns cannot be attributed to advertising.)

Q5. What do you mean by copy testing? What are the techniques used in it?

Ans. Copy testing is normally done before the campaign starts. Questions like: Will a proposed copy theme be effective at achieving advertising objectives? Does the set of advertisements that make up an advertising campaign create the desired interest level and image? Will an individual advertisement attract the attention of the audience?, are answered by copy testing.

This research is done to find out whether the creatives' used will have the desired effect on the audience or not. An entire category of copy testing is designed primarily not to test the impact of a total ad but to help creative people understand how parts of the ad contribute to its impact. Techniques used in this are given below:

Oualitative Research: Focus groups research is widely used at the front end of the development of an advertising campaign.

Audience Impressions of the ad: Many copy tests add a set of open-ended questions to the procedures designed to tap the audience's impressions of what the ad was about, what ideas were presented, interest in the ideas, and so on.

Adjective checklists: This uses a checklist questionnaire which includes adjectives that allow advertiser to determine how warm, amusing, irritated or informative the respondent it to be. Several of these checklist contain phrases like: "I can see myself doing that....", "I can relate to that...", and so on.

Physiological measures: Several kinds of instruments are used to observe reactions to advertisements. In general, they attempt to capture the changes in nervous system or emotional arousal during exposure sequence. Gadgets used primarily consist of eye camera, pupillometrics and Conpaad.

Q6. What are the syndicated and custom research techniques?

Ans. A number of syndicated research services specialise in the evaluation of individual advertisements and, on occasion, advertising campaigns. Because these services vary so greatly in methodology, we are only covering the major ones.

(1) Television Rating Points (TVRs): This research is used in measurement of television audience. In India, as of now, two companies do this kind of research. The viewership measurement is specific to the time bands. Usefulness of this research is that it helps in formulation of media plans. Advertising campaigns can benefit from perfect targeting by using this research.

(2) Press Readership: Comparable of Television Rating Points is readership survey (IRS 1998). This reassert is used in measurement of readership of various print vehicles. Again, like TVRs this research helps in perfect targeting. This research is used primarily while doing, media planning for a campaign.

As far as custom research are concerned there are many existing today in the market. Various research companies have developed their own models and offer to do research for advertisers on the basis of their models. For example, one of the research company offers following research services:

Add+Impact: This is a pre-testing and evaluation system. It uses qualitative and quantitative approach to measure the emotional pre-disposition of consumers towards creative idea.

Ideamap: A computer based product optimisation system that goes towards understanding and gauging from among many concepts options to arrive at an optimal combination of concept elements and allows fine tuning for maximum impact towards making a campaign effective.

(3) Starch Tests: This is a form of media research done to find out the impact of placing (position) of the advertisements on different pages of a publication. Starch measures three degree of readership:

- **Noted:** The percentage who remember having previously seen the advertisement in the issue or a publication;
- **Associated:** The percentage who saw any part of the ad that clearly indicates the brand or advertiser; and
- **Read Most:** The percentage who read 50% or more of the written material in the advertisement.

Starch test throws light on the correct sise of the advertisements, difference on impact in cases of left hand page v/s right hands, page, difference on impact when using a colour advertisement and a B&W advertisement.

Chapter-8

Measuring Advertising Effectiveness: Definition and Techniques

Q1. What is the objective of advertising campaign?

Ans. Advertising objectives are the communication tasks to be accomplished with specific customers that a company is trying to reach during a particular time frame. A company that advertises usually strives to achieve one of four advertising objectives: trial, continuity, brand switching, and switchback. Which of the four advertising objectives is selected usually depends on where the product is in its life cycle.

(1) Trial: The purpose of the trial objective is to encourage customers to make an initial purchase of a new product. Companies will typically employ creative advertising strategies in order to cut through other competing advertisements. The reason is simple: Without that first trial of a product by customers, there will not be any repeat purchases.

(2) Continuity: Continuity advertising is a strategy to keep current customers using a particular product. Existing customers are targeted and are usually provided new and different information about a product that is designed to build consumer loyalty.

(3) Brand Switching: Companies adopt brand switching as an objective when they want customers to switch from competitors' brands to their brands. A common strategy is for a company to compare product price or quality in order to convince customers to switch to its product brand. Switchback - Companies subscribe to this advertising objective when they want to get back former users of their product brand. A company might highlight new product features, price reductions, or other important product information in order to get former customers of its product to switchback.

Q2. Methods used for measuring effective advertising?

Ans. Advertising is not only aimed in improving the sales volume but it also create the brand image of the company. On the basis of quantitative and qualitative parameters, there are two types' measures, direct measures and, indirect measures.

(1) Direct Measures of Advertising Effectiveness: Under direct measures, a relationship between advertising and sales is established. A comparison of sales of two periods or two periods or two markets may be done and the corresponding changes may be noted. The following are some of the methods that are generally used in measuring that advertising effects.

- **Historical Sales Method**: Some insights into the effectiveness of past advertising may be obtained by measuring the relationship between the advertising expenditure and the total sales of the product. A multiple regression analysis of advertising expenditure and sales over several time periods may be calculated. It would show how the changes in advertising expenditure have corresponding changes in sales volume. This technique estimates the contribution that advertising has made to explaining in a co relational manner rather than a casual sales, the variation in sales over the time periods covered in the study

- **Experimental Control**: The other measure of advertising effectiveness is the method of experimental control where a casual relationship between advertising and sales is established. This method is quite expensive when related to other advertising effectiveness measures yet it is possible to isolate advertising contribution to sales. Moreover this can be done as a pre-test to aid advertising in choosing between alternative creative designs. Media schedules expenditure levels or some combination of these advertising decision areas. One experimental approach to measuring the sales effectiveness of advertising is test marketing.

(2) Indirect Measures of Advertising Effectiveness: As it is very difficult to measure the direct effect of advertising on company's profits or sales, most firms rely heavily on indirect measures. These measures do not evaluate the effects of advertisements directing on sales or profits but all other factors such as customer awareness or attitude or customer recall of advertising message affect the sales or profits or goals of the business indirectly. Despite the uncertainties about the relationship between the intermediate effects of advertising and the ultimate results, there is no other alternative but to use indirect measures. The most commonly used measures are;

- **Exposure to Advertisement**: In order to be effective, the advertisement must gain exposure. The management is concerned about the number of target audiences who see or hear the organisation message set in the advertisement. Without exposure, advertisement is bound to failure. Marketers or advertisers may obtain an idea of exposure generated by the medium by examining its circulation or audience data which reveal the number of copies of the magazine, newspaper or journal sold the number of persons passing the billboards or riding in transit facilities, or the number of persons living in the televiewing or radio listening area, and the number of persons switching on their T.V. and radio sets at various points of time. This number can be estimated by interviewing the numbers of the audience for different media.

- **Attention or Recall of Advertising Message Content**: This is one of the widely used measures of advertising results. Under this measure, a recall of the message content among a specified group or groups or prospective customers is measured within 24 hours of the exposure of the advertisement. Attention value is the chief quality of the advertising copy the advertisements cannot be said to be effective unless they attract the attention of the target consumers. There are two methods for evaluating the attention getting value of the advertisements. One is pre-test and the other is post-test. In a pre-test evaluation, the consumers are asked to indicate the extent to which they recognise or recall the advertisement, they have already seen. This test is conducted in the laboratory setting. Here consumers read, hear or listen to the advertisement and then researchers ask question regarding the advertisement just to test the recall and then evaluate it. In post-test method, the consumers are asked questions about the indication of recognition or recall after the advertisement has been run. These measures assume that customers can recall or recognise what they have viewed or listened to. Various mechanical devices are being used in the western countries which provide indices of attention such as eye-camera etc.

- **Brand Awareness:** The marketers who rely heavily on advertising often appraise its effectiveness by measuring the customer's awareness about the particular product or brand. The assumption of this type of measure is that there is a direct relationship between the advertisements and the awareness. This type of measure is also subject to the same criticisms as is applicable to direct measures of effectiveness (sales measures because awareness is also not the direct result of the advertisements. It is also affected by many other factors. But, for new products, changes in awareness can often be attributed to the influence of advertising.

- **Comprehension:** Consumers generally use advertisements as a means of obtaining information about the product, brand or the manufacturer. They cannot be informed unless they comprehend the message (grasp the message mentally and understand it fully). Various tests for valuating comprehension are available. One is recall tests – an indicator of comprehension because it is evident that consumers recall what they comprehend. Another measure of the variable is to ask questions about subjects how much they have comprehended a message they have recently heard or seen. One may employ somewhat imprecise test of the comprehension of a newspaper and radio advertisement. One may ask typical target consumers from time to time such questions like 'what did you think of our new commercial?' and 'Did it get the message across'? The answers of these questions will provide sufficient insight into advertising decision making.

- **Attitude Change:** Since advertising is considered to be one way of influencing the state of the mind of the audience towards a product, service or organisation, the results are very often measured in terms of attitudes among groups exposed to advertising communication. Several measures are used ranging from asking the questions about willingness to buy the likelihood of buying to the measurement of the extent to which specific attributes (such as modern or new) are associated with a product.

- **Action:** One objective of advertisement may be assumed to be to stimulate action or behavior. The action or intention to take an action may be measured on the intention to buy measuring instrument. Under this type of measure, consumers are asked to respond why they are interested in purchasing the product or brand. One type of action that advertisers attempt to induce is buying behavior. The assumption is that if an increase in sales follows a decrease in advertising expenditure, the change in sales levels are good indicators of the effectiveness of advertising. Logic suggests that measurement of sales is preferable to other measurements.

Thus, these above measures (direct or indirect) are used to evaluate the effectiveness of advertisements. It seems from the analysis of the above methods of measuring effectiveness that directly or indirectly changes in sales or profits are taken as the measuring rod of the effectiveness of the advertising.

Q3. Importance of measuring the Effectiveness of Advertising?

Ans. It acts as a Safety measure: Testing effectiveness of advertising helps in finding out ineffective advertisement and advertising campaigns. It facilitates timely adjustments in advertising to make advertising consumer oriented and result oriented. Thus waste of money in faulty advertising can be avoided.

Provides feedback for remedial measures: Testing effectiveness of advertising provides useful information to the advertisers to take remedial steps against ineffective advertisements.

Avoids possible failure: Advertisers are not sure of results of advertising from a particular advertising campaign. Evaluating advertising effectives helps in estimating the results in order to avoid complete loss.

To justify the Investment in Advertising: The expenditure on advertisement is considered to be an investment. The investment in advertising is a marketing investment and its objectives should be spelt out clearly indicating the results expected from the campaign. The rate and sise of return should be determined in advance. If the expected rate of return is achieved in terms of additional profits, the advertisement can be considered as effective one.

To know the communication Effect: The effectiveness of the advertisement can be measured in terms of their communication effects on the target consumers or audience. The main purpose of advertising is communicated the general public, and existing and prospective consumers, various information about the product and the company. It is therefore desirable to seek post measurements of advertising in order to determine whether advertisement have been seen or heard or in other words whether they have communicated the theme, message or appeal of the advertising.

Compare two markets: Under this procedure, advertising is published in test markets and results are contrasted with other. Markets – so called control markets – which have had the regular advertising program. The measurements made to determine results may be measurements of change in sales, change in consumer attitudes, changes in dealer display and so on depending upon the objectives sought by the advertiser.

❏❏❏

Chapter-9

Media Concepts, Characteristics and Issues in Media Planning

Q1. What is all about advertising plan and its role?

Ans. As soon as the term marketing & advertising arises the confusion begins because more or less they both are similar on few things but having many differences like, advertising can create the awareness among the customer and marketing can increase the sale of the product. On the other hand we can say that marketing is sales oriented and advertising is communication oriented. Therefore, the task of advertising is to create the most effective and distinctive communication in the marketplace, which can be expressed in form of three brand objectives:-

- Brand Growth (launched of new brand)
- Brand Share Maintenance (established brand)
- Protection from in roads (wherein one brand tries to stay off competition)

Role of Advertising:
- **Vehicle of Direct Impact:** Its first motive is to generate the need of product or service in the mind of the customer, so they say "I must buy now". Example TATA Nano advertisement
- **A Tool of Seeking Information:** Secondly it can create the curiosity in the mind of the customer who says "I must find out". Example Iphone advertisement
- **A Link between Communication & Consumer Needs:** It gives the knowledge and information about product and service in the market which can fulfill customer needs and wants. Example Home Loans advertisement

- **A Tool that Aims to Modify Attitudes:** It helps in changing the image or perception of the product or service in the customer's eyes Example Coca Cola advertisement after controversy
- **Vehicle to Reinforce the Attitude:** In this cut throat competitive environment it is important for the company to highlight its product and service in the customers mind. Example Hamara Baja advertisement.

Q2. What are the methods used in setting the advertising budget?

Ans. Marketers believe that advertising helps in increasing the demand for a product in the market. The amount of money spent on an advertising campaign should be in accordance with the sales it generates. The budget of an advertisement varies depending on the stage of lifecycle of the product. For an example new product may need huge budget as it has to create awareness about the product and encourage the potential customer to buy.

Setting an advertising budget is a difficult task because marketers cannot quantify the benefits accruing from an advertisement or determine the exact sales an advertisement has generated. Some common thumb rules (like advertising/sales ratio) or methods followed by firms are:-

(1) Objective and Task Method: It is one of the rational approaches to setting advertising budget, the method by which the budget developed are:-
- Defining their specific advertising objective,
- Determining the task that must be performed to achieve those objective, and
- Estimating the cost of performing those task.

The sum total of all these costs determines the advertising budget. The major disadvantage of using this method is that marketers cannot accurately estimate or quantify the efforts required to achieve an objective.

(2) Percent-of-sales-method: It can be expressed by a formula: (Spending on advertisement in rupees/Sales in rupees)*100

It is developed by studying the past records of sales figure and budget allocation, which can give the repetition of the past performance. Projecting the product's sales for the current year is very important and for doing so, understanding the market scenario and predicting competitor strategies is vital.

(3) Affordability Method: In this method, a marketer, after allocating all other expenses in his budget, allocates the remaining funds to advertising. This method does prevent a drain on cash flow, but it disregards the correlation between the advertising expenditure and the sales result. Likewise, during recession, funds are not available with the marketers and therefore, they reduce the advertising expenditure, which further reduces future sales.

(4) Competitive Parity Method: In this companies allocate advertising budget by comparing with competitors advertising budget. The advertising budget of a company may match with that of a competitor either in rupee term or in term of percent-of-sales. If companies follow this method, it must have the collective knowledge of the industry to arrive at a figure for its advertising budget. In this method companies need to be very careful because their objective and available resources may be totally different.

Q3. Write down the types of media.
Or
What do you mean by media characteristic?

Ans. The word media comes from the Latin word "middle." Media carry messages from source to destination. There are basically two type of media for communication, mass media and inter-personal media, they both are different and cannot be used as one substituting the other.

(1) Mass media: It is a technological base medium for transferring the message; hence it is cost effective and covers the wide area. The only drawback with it, it's a one way communication, which is impersonal. It is further divided in to five parts which are as follows:-

(2) Interpersonal Media: It is a medium in which personal meeting is required, hence it is a two way communication, it is costly but gives the proper and immediate feedback. These kinds of media are useful at the time of new product launch, social campaign, or at the industrial product launch. The various kind of interpersonal media are as follows:-

Q4. Write down the advance methods of media communication.
Or
What are the Merits & Demerits of the print & electronic media?
Ans. (1) Newspaper

Merits: High coverage, Low cost, Short lead time for placing ads, Ads can placed in interest sections, Timely (current ads), Reader controls exposure, Can be used for coupons.

Demerits: Short life, Clutter, Low attention-getting capabilities, Poor reproduction quality, Selective reader exposure

(2) Magazine:

Merits: Segmentation potential, Quality reproduction, High information content, Longevity, Multiple readers

Demerits: Long lead time for ad placement, Visual only, Lack of flexibility

(3) Television:

Merits: Mass coverage, High reach, Impact of sight, sound, and motion, High prestige, Low cost per exposure, Attention getting, Favorable mage.

Demerits: Low selectivity, Short message life, High absolute cost, High production costs, Clutter.

(4) Radio:

Merits: Local coverage, Low cost, High frequency, Flexible, Low production costs, Well-segmented audiences.

Demerits: Audio only, Clutter, Low attention getting, Fleeting message.

(5) Direct Mail:

Merits: High selectivity, Reader controls exposure, High information content, Opportunities for repeat exposures.

Demerits: High cost/contact, Poor image (junk mail), Clutter.

(6) Posters:

Merits: Graphic opportunities, color, Large sise, High-fidelity reproduction, Simple, direct approach, possibility of a total visual message.

Demerits: A one line medium, with limited opportunity of advertisement expansion, Inadequate audience research, especially in transit advertising.

(7) Point of Sale:

Merits: Opportunity for three-dimensional effect, Movement sound and innovative production techniques.

Demerits: Difficult in analysing the audience, Failure of retailer to make proper use of material submitted to them.

Q5. How one can evaluate the available media option & why it is necessary?

Ans. Critically analyse the advantages and disadvantages of each marketing communications media variable and advertising media options for a product or service

Determine media characteristics that match the requirements of the advertising brief for the product or service.

Analyse media consumption habits for primary and supplementary advertising media among target audiences.

Select advertising media options that match the requirements of the advertising brief for the product or service.

Evaluate media styles as they relate to brand character of product/service being advertised.

Compare the advantages and disadvantages of selecting multiple media in a media plan.

Develop and apply criteria for multiple media combination selection.

Recommend a primary advertising media which meets target audience preferences.

Select and recommend supplementary media to complement the primary medium.

Ensure recommended media meet the advertising brief and advertiser's requirements and legal and ethical constraints.

The advantage in following is that the brands will be easily identified with the image of the program which it is trying to create.

Q6. What are the factors to be considered during media selection?

Ans. The problem of selection of the best medium or media for a particular advertiser will vary greatly, depending on the particular situation, circumstances and different other factors in which a person in conducting individual business. Media selection involves a number of major factors which influence the decision of the advertiser. The most significant of these factors are:

1. The nature of the product
2. Potential market
3. The type of distribution strategy
4. The advertising objective
5. The type of selling message
6. The budget
7. Competitive advertising
8. Media Availability.
9. Characteristics of media

Gullybaba.com

Simply Scan QR Codes to Jump at Our Latest Products

HELP BOOKS

TYPED ASSIGNMENTS

HAND WRITTEN ASSIGNMENTS

READYMADE PROJECTS

CUSTOMIZED PROJECTS

COMBOS OF BOOKS/ ASSIGNMENTS

Note: The above QR Codes can be scanned and open through QR Code Scanner Application/App of your smart mobile Phone.

Chapter-10

Media Selection, Planning and Scheduling

Q1. What do you mean by the term media?
Ans. Communication is a two way process where messages flow both ways. Communication also refers to that use of different forms of media, such as print, electronic media (radio, television), new media etc. It has the strong emphasis of communication between the targeted audience and company. It is consisted of tangible elements like which we can see, feel, hear & react to.

Types of media: newspaper, magazine, radio, television, directory (yellow pages), direct mail media, point of purchase, outdoor media, transit media, screen media, specialty media.

Q2. Explain media planning process
Ans. It is a process of designing and scheduling a plan of advertising time, space, its medium or media vehicle through which the organisation can achieve its marketing objective. Media planning is a very important component of the marketing strategy of every company. On the other hand we can say that it is a important tool of the marketing strategy through which it can select the appropriate media to communicate its message without any interruption to the maximum number of its potential customer. Media planning helps to control wastage in advertising. It ensures the optimum utilisation of resources spent on advertising.

Media planning is similar to the blueprint of advertising programs of the company. To obtain this blueprint, the company must involve in many activities that are related to the firms marketing activities. Scopes of the media plan are as follows:

(1) Situation Analysis: Strategy & targets (business/brand/consumer), Market situation and competition analysis, Marketing and media objectives.

(2) Objectives: The objective of the advertising, can be for the awareness of the new product or services, or to recall the existing product or service which is improved. The objective can for interest generation, brand positioning, brand development, brand management, or to create purchase intentions, customer loyalty

(3) Target group analysis: Target group identification: two-step segmentation process, definition of core target groups based on demographic characteristics (age, gender), psychographic characteristics (interests, buying habits), socioeconomic characteristics (occupation, social status, income, buying power), behavioral characteristics (buying behavior, decision behavior)

(4) Strategic media planning: Campaign strategy (duration, timing, recency/burst strategy), Media mix and budgeting, advertising impact, Ad specials

(5) Detail planning: Detail planning for each media channel, Availability, Dates of publication, Selection of time slots, Positioning within the magazine or commercial break

(6) Purchasing: Booking (order management, production plans), Job handling (artwork, tapes), Rescheduling/Optimisation

(7) Completion: Controlling, documentation, Invoicing

(8) Evaluation/Controlling: Campaign performance (expert analysis), Planning, purchasing efficiency, Competition reporting

Q3. Write down the process of media selection.

Ans. As we know that media planning helps us to find the right time, space and different media for advertising to achieve the marketing and advertising objective of the company. So the basic goal of its to find out best suitable combination of media to communicate the message in the most effective manner but at lower cost, this is done by only advertiser or by the advertising company. The plan is decided by the advertiser keeping in view the marketing objective of the company. Media plan is based on advertising plan. In other words we can say media plan is a part of the overall advertising plan. The selection process deals with a series of question that need to be answered in the pursuit of media selection.

Who should be reached?: Identification of the target segment is dependent on the market segmentation. Segmentation on the basis of customer demographics, psychographics, social class, product usage and so on will help the media planner reach the maximum number of customer in those segment, within the budget constraints.

Where they are located?: Advertising must ideally be targeted at place where most of the potential buyers are located. Differences in tastes and preferences exist for various products, based on the geographic location. For an example, demand for the tea is higher than for coffee in north India and the reverse is true for south India. Available of a medium also has some geographic limitations. The advertiser should identify the location of his target audience and accordingly advertise in local or national media.

Which medium is appropriate?: The message that has to be delivered is very critical for the selection of the medium. A particular type of message requires a particular type of medium. If a new product is to be launched in the market, a feeling of something new and exciting should be created and that can be effectively done by using the newspaper, the radio and the television. If the product or service needs a demonstration, then a television ad would be more appropriate then a print advertisement. If a high quality output in a color is required, then multicolored magazines would do the job better when compared to newspaper. If there has been a controversy and the company wants to rebuild the lost confidence of customer in its brand or product, it can be communicate its stand through the print media to show the proof or evidence, certifying the quality of the product. If there is a need to build the brand image of a company on the basis of some personality traits, then can be advertised during relevant program on television or radio. For example advertisement related to health drink is aired on television during children program telecasting time.

When do we run the advertising campaign?: Advertising message can be aired any time during the year depending upon the product or service. Normally the timing of the advertisement can be decided on the basis of the season, months, weeks, days, and even minutes and seconds. For example water heater advertisement during winter season. Apart from seasonal product there are a host of the products that would benefits from different timed advertisement. For example MRF ads are aired when Sachin Tendulkar, its major endorser is batting. While deciding, when to advertise, the type of audience also plays a significant role.

Q4. What is media scheduling?

Ans. Media scheduling means the outline of time in which the advertisement is going to be run. Basically it is for fixing up the time slots according to the advertiser so that the message delivered can reach to the target audience properly on time. There are three types of scheduling which are as follows:

(1) Continuity: This type of scheduling is best for the products which are not depending upon season. They can be run throughout the year with the fixed intervals. It is basically use as the reminder for the product. It helps in maintaining continues and complete purchase cycle having a regular demand over the year. There can be a Rising Continuity in which some specific products are been advertised in the peak seasons for e.g. floaters are advertised more in rainy season while some products fall under a Falling Continuity in which either ads for new products are run or if there is any other change in the existing product. E.g. packaging of Pediasure, a kid's health drink is recently changed

(2) Flighting: It is also known as bursting. This is an absolute season based product model. The advertisement runs at very irregular intervals or for a very shorter period. Because the advertisement is for limited time or occasionally they are in the concentrated form hence less waste of funds. The best media type for such scheduling is television and radio. So the advertisers who cannot afford the year long ads, this is a best option. For example advertisements for warm clothes in Indian Market.

(3) Pulsing: It is a combination of both continuity and flighting. In this advertisement run whole year but less in number, and heavy advertisement are preferred at the peak time. Generally scheduling is fixed for a month. There are six types of scheduling method here.

- Steady pulse has fixed schedule for example one advertisement per week for 52 week or one advertisement per month for 12 months.
- Seasonal pulse has bunches of advertisement season wise.
- Period pulse are regular basis advertisements but not related to the season.
- Erratic pulse refers to irregular ads normally used for changing old patterns.
- Start up pulse is used for new product with heavy advertisements.
- Promotional pulse refers to short period single use ads used basically for promoting products or events.

Q5. What type of Segmentation can be done in Media planning?

Ans. A market comprises of different consumers possessing innumerable tastes and preferences. Depending on their marketing approach and the nature of the product, marketers can adopt different levels of segmentation. The levels of market segmentation are:-

(1) National Level Segmentation: It most likely by the marketers, those who are marketing national brands, the national plan seeks to reach the masses. For this the national newspaper and magazine is select as the key media vehicle.

(2) Key Market Segmentation: In the case of national brands and regional brands, media strategists seek to cover effectively the key markets rather than spread over the entire market. This plan is most needed at the introduction stages of the product life -cycle (PLC). It is also required for those products that have regional formulations to suit regional, climatic conditions. Regional newspapers are the major media vehicle for this.

(3) Skim Segmentation: As key market media plans concentrate on geographic areas, skim plans aim at a market from a demographic or psychographic perspective. In these plans, the markets first aim to skim off the cream of a segment and then sell it in general to the other markets.

Q6. What are the elements to develop media strategy?

Ans. The basic elements of Media Strategy are as follows:

- **Media Mix:** Combination of media to be used in an advertising campaign. In the past, television and magazines dominated the media mixes of most national advertising campaigns because these media reached the broadest segments of the market. In present scenario media mixes now include vehicles such as telephone directories, cable television, ballpark billboards, supermarket shopping carts, and other forms of media that may reach a narrower market segment but cost less and target more effectively

- **Usage of Media:** Each medium lends itself for use in various ways, by way of commercial forms in which it is available. How each is to be used in terms of spot buying vs. sponsorship on television, time/space units general interest vs. special interest publications, prime time/space vs. non-prime time/space, color vs. black & white, main issue vs. supplements and so on – are decisions to be taken so as to extract the best mileage out of the selected media.

- **Geographic Allocation:** According to the market priorities in different geographic location different media are used. The advertising company has to allocate the proper media mix for different location.

- **Scheduling Strategy:** The extent and spacing of the media activity in a time frame is expostulated. Rationales for controlling the continuity of the exposures are also provided. These are dependent upon various factors drawn from various background analyses done earlier on seasonality, competitive advertising, budgetary considerations, brand purchase cycle and so on.

Chapter-11

Internet as an Emerging Advertising Medium

Q1. What are application available on Internet for marketing?

Ans. The internet has become a revolution in marketing. Certain methods such as bulk email cost you next to nothing, but can increase sales.

- **Bulk Email Marketing:** If you already have a large number of subscribers to your business mailing list, you don't need to spend much to reach a targeted audience - just think of an offer that your customers would have trouble resisting, and send them an email. The bulk emailer system allows you to see who responded to your offer - who opened the email, and what link did they click? This is useful information as it enables you to re-focus your efforts for future mail outs. A big advantage of bulk email is the very low cost of reaching people that have indicated they are interested in your offerings.

- **Search Engine Optimisation:** It relies on providing more details to search engines so that your product and service content is more useful to your visitors than your competitor's web sites.

- **Social Media Marketing:** People like spending a lot of their time on social media sites, and with a clever campaign you can reach an enormous number. For example, Face Book

- **Pay Per Click Marketing:** A way of getting new clients on to your subscriber list is to use Pay Per Click advertising, still a targeted means of getting your offer in front of potential new clients. This is more expensive, as you have to pay the advertising network (such as Google, Facebook or Bing) for every click, but if you think about it long term, you're aquiring new email contacts as well, so the cost of re-marketing to these clients drops over time.

Q2. What are the difference between Traditional and Internet Advertising?

Ans. The internet has become a medium for advertising. It has also been favored by consumers and businessmen in public shopping and business dealings. Unlike any other media, like television, radio and print, internet advertising solutions with its low cost has become extensively used. It could capture texts, images, video and audio. Usually advertisers could produce logos, moving banners, animated and 3d imagery. With these in hand, advertisers mix these forms to produce successful and low cost internet advertising solutions.

The only is not that it is reasonable, internet advertising solution serve as a communication station; it also assists in an easy system for transaction and distribution. This is the only medium that could help people do business within a small period of time. With just one click and a money-saving internet advertising solution, shoppers could get all the information they need by visiting any web site. The businessman could get the services he needs. The company is happy doing business with their clients. The clients are happy doing business in the ease of their homes. Generally meeting person will need the time and money could be wasted, the low cost internet advertising solutions benefits the company in which the services and products are receiving sales and also customer get the maximum satisfaction.

Low-cost internet advertising solutions are able to guide other advertising medium because they were developed to be interactive. When a consumer reads and clicks on a web advertisement, it is easier and more convenient to respond or inquire with e-mail and business reply cards. Unlike other advertisings, low cost internet advertising solutions' capability to answer feed backs in real time enables the companies to reply, resolves complaints and answer inquiries. Internet advertising solutions provide a low cost and effective resolution for attracting targeted, high quality customers. But conventional advertising could never be replaced. However, because of developments in the technology, people prefer their services online. With low cost internet advertising solutions present, the consumers, companies, advertisers and even the common people's lives have been given a deserving contentment.

Q3. What are the similarities between internet and mass media advertising?

Ans. Both types of media can be saved for future reference. People can cut clippings from newspapers and magazines or save a web page to view at a later time. In contrast, other media such as radio is perishable, as the audiences have no opportunity to save the audio; instead they have to remember it or wait for it to be played again.

Online media can present the audience with information as soon as it is available. With the advances in technology many people can now access the Internet on their mobile phones, which grants them access to online media anytime and anywhere. On the other hand, print media has to go through the printing process before it is available to its audience. This is not necessarily a weakness, however, as it allow editors to check the validity of the information and produce a more developed text.

Why Students Choose GPH Books

- Syllabus covered as prescribed by Universities/Boards/Institutions.
- Easily understandable language and format that help students prepare for exam in short period of time.
- Published with exam-oriented approach, hence prepared in question-answer format which provides students the instant understanding of a correct answer.
- Maximum solved previous year question papers included which help students to understand unique examination structure and equip them better for exam.
- Both semesters' question papers (June-December) are included with solutions.
- Instant updation of data as and when any change occurs.
- Use of recycled paper.
- Handy books and reasonable prices.
- For every book sold, we contribute for society/institution/NGOs/underprivileged

Chapter-12

Managing Sales Promotion

Q1. What are the various methods for consumer sales promotion?

Ans. Marketers use sales promotion to introduce a new product or brand, or promote the existing brand. On the other hand retailer uses sales promotion to attract customer to their stores. They can use a number of sales promotion tools to boost their sales which are as follows:-

- **Price Promotion:** Price promotion is also commonly known as price discounting. They offer either a discount on the normal selling price of the product or more of the product at the same price. This type of promotion must be used with care as the increase in sale is gained at the cost of a loss in the profit. Also too much of discounting can have a negative impact on the brand's reputation.

- **Coupons:** Offering coupons is the most widely used customer sales promotion technique. It is yet another way of offering a discount. A coupon is a certificate that offers a price reduction for some specified items to the holder. Coupons are distributed along with magazine, newspaper etc.

- **Free gifts/samples:** Free samples of a new product are usually given to customers, when it is launched in the market. Gift with purchase is a very common promotional technique. It is also known as premium promotion as the customer gets something in addition to the main purchase. Offering free gifts or samples is the most expensive form of sales promotion. Marketers use this technique to increase their sales volume in the early stages of the product life cycle.

This type of promotion is widely used for subscription based products (like magazines, etc), and for consumer luxuries (like perfumes, vehicles etc).

- **Money refunds and rebates:** In this the customer receives a specific amount of money (as refund) after he submits a proof of purchase to the manufacturer. Manufacturer develops the strategy such that the customer qualifies for a refund only when he makes multiple purchases. But in some cases, marketers refund cash to customer on making a single purchase. These schemes are often viewed with some suspicion, especially if the method of obtaining a refund looks unusual. The customer might even doubt the manufacturer's reason for offering rebates and refunds. This can lead to a degradation of the brand's image, if the scheme is not handled properly.

- **Frequent user incentives:** Repeat purchase may be stimulated by frequent user incentives. Hence firm offer incentives schemes to reward their loyal customer.

- **Point-of-purchase display:** It work as silent sales force. In which window displays, display racks, danglers, balloons, outside sign, counter pieces and innovations such as sniff teasers that spread products aroma in the stores etc. are used. These items often provided by the manufacturer, to encourage the retailer, so that he stores the product in his store, to attract the attention of a customer and inform him about the product. Research on customer buying behavior in retail stores suggests that a significant proportion of purchase result from displays that customer come across in the store. Attractive, information and well positioned point-of-purchase displays therefore from an important part of sales promotion.

- **Installment offers:** Manufacturer as well as retailer offer products at a down payment and allow the customer durable and white goods use this type of promotional method.

- **Consumer contest:** This method of sales promotion is carried out when a marketer aims at increasing the retail sale of a product. Customer takes part in small competitions on the basis of their creative and analytical skill. Such contests attract customer's attention. However, marketers should take care in designing a contest as dissatisfied customer can stop purchasing the firm's product or speak negatively about the company to their reference group. And at times, they may even resort to litigation.

- **Consumer sweepstakes:** In this type so sales promotion, customers are required to submit their names to be include in a draw for prise, sweepstakes are more profitable in comparison to contests, as the chances of lawsuits are minimal and they attract a vast majority of customer. Sweepstakes can help in generating customer interest in the product and also lead to short-term increase in sales.
- **Trade shows:** A group of retailers or manufacturers conduct exhibitions and trade shows to make the customer aware of the products offered by various firms.

Q2. What are the various methods for trade sales promotion?

Ans. Manufacturer use special trade promotion methods to encourage resellers like wholesaler, distributor, and retailers etc. to promote their products. They might use a number of methods to attract the middlemen, like trade shows, premiums, sales contest, etc. The methods through which the sales promotion can be done are as follows:-

- **Buying allowance:** It is a method in which the temporary price reduction is been done on the product and offers to the retailer for purchasing a specific quantity of the product. Such an offer acts as an incentive to stimulate short-term profit of the retailers and promote new products for the company.
- **Buyback allowance:** In this kind of sales promotion, the channel members are offered a monetary incentives for each additional unit purchased after the initial deal. This method aims at stimulating the channel member to purchase additional quantities of stock that is over and above the normal stocks, as the monetary incentive they receive is proportional to the amount of additional stock they purchase.
- **Merchandise allowance:** In this type of trade promotion, a manufacturer agrees to pay the reseller certain amount of money for promoting the company's product through advertising or display. Middleman is usually required to show the proof of the advertisement carried out by them.
- **Free merchandise:** It is a technique in which an additional amount of the product is offered without any additional cost, as

an incentive to purchase a minimum quantity. The incentive is typically offered for a limited period of time.

- **Dealer loader:** It is a reward or gift, which is a part of the display kit given to the retailer, to encourage him to display the merchandise. Retailers obtain gift only when they buy specific quantities of goods and retain the gift when the promotion is over. This is used at the time of making new distributors or they want to push product to retailer.

- **Dealer listing:** It is a technique in which the advertisement of a company identifies and acknowledges its retailers. Dealer listings help in persuading the retailer to carry the product and also encourage the customer to buy the product at a particular dealer's outlet.

- **Scan back allowance:** It is aimed specifically at retail outlet. Retailers are rewarded on the basis of the number of units that moved through their scanners or hand-held wants during a specific time. To participate in these program retailers has to reduce the retail price or offer special prices on a given product for a specific time period.

Chapter-13

Direct Marketing

Q1. What is direct marketing, explain its growth and characteristics?
Ans. In direct marketing companies reach their customer directly without any intermediary through a medium, which may be the internet, telephone, post etc. Marketers try to market their products by reaching the customers through such direct forms of marketing, and to persuade them to buy their products or services. There are various methods marketers adopts for direct marketing such as catalog marketing, telemarketing, kiosk marketing, home shopping etc. Direct marketing is similar to traditional marketing activities except that is has following three additional features:

- In direct marketing, marketers invite customers to respond to their marketing efforts through the telephone, email etc.
- The effectiveness of direct marketing can be measured easily because direct feedback is available to marketers from customer.
- In this a database of a customer is maintained. This helps marketers understand customers and serve them better, and ultimately gives the marketer a competitive advantage.

Direct marketing evaluates the direct response patterns of customer, enables a company to formulate future marketing strategies for building customer loyalty and for profitable business growth. The growth of direct marketing is phenomenal, beginning with conventional telephonic sales; direct marketing has now taken off on a global scale, as companies around the world are using web technologies to make their marketing programs more effective. Email marketing, web based marketing and other such marketing moves have become important elements of marketing today, in which the effective marketing research studies also helped.

Direct marketing is growing at a very fast pace, and it helps marketers target the desire segment efficiently.

The key characteristics of direct marketing which distinguished it's from all other marketing methods is its efficiency. In this we can determine the success or failure of any effort by testing it on the small scale and reduce the wastage of the budget and can also control the situation. Through this we can personalise the message according to the target audience and can have the immediate response. In direct marketing we are have one more benefit that is of database through which we can recall the prospect customer. As direct marketing can be done through email, telephone, home shopping portals it can overcome the problem of physical presence and the geographical limitations too.

Q2. What are different types of direct marketing tools used by the marketers?

Ans. There are various forms of direct marketing which are as follows:

(1) Catalog marketing: It is a process in which companies send their catalogs containing details of products and services to customers and expect them to respond by placing orders by telephone or by mails. It is a convenient way for customers to purchase the product and advantageous for retailers, so they operate from remote location with minimum store operating expenses and need not spend heavy amount on store décor. Catalog marketing is suitable for a limited range of product. It helps companies reduce their cost per customer and increase their reach significantly, because marketers first evaluate the customer whether he would like to buy the product on the given price or not.

(2) Telemarketing: It is a process of communicating with customer through the telephone, to promote product or service. It required highly trained marketing staff to whom specific objectives is given. Telemarketing is usually aimed at people who are prospective customer and require the service offered by a marketer. Its aimed for long-term relationship with customer rather than making immediate sales like telesales. Most of the companies provide the toll-free number for customer respond. Telemarketing helps marketers build positive relationship with their customer, understand their needs better and develop new products according to the requirements of prospective customer. There are various objectives of telemarketing efforts, such as developing customer loyalty, conducting market research, generating leads, etc.

(3) Kiosk marketing: This kind of marketing involves the use of kiosks or electronic touch screens, which provide information to customers regarding products and services of a company. The uses of kiosks are beneficial for customer because they can be set up at places convenient for them, and enable them to obtain relevant information about the company without visiting the company. It can be set up at a very small place, and can be operated by 24*7 without any supervision. The live example for kiosks is railways ticketing.

(4) Homeshopping: It is generally done through television and internet in which various products are displayed and their uses are demonstrated to viewers. Order can be placed by the viewer through phone or mail. Once the order is placed, these products are delivered to the customer within two to three weeks, normally with a cash-on-delivery option. The increase in the popularity of home shopping is attributed to the customer's perception of low prices, better after-sales services, cash-on-delivery option, easy monthly installments and polite and informed sales person.

Q3. What mediums are used for the direct marketing?
Ans. Direct marketing can be effectively done through newspaper, magazines, journals, company newsletters, post cards, postal envelops, leaflets and doo-to-door selling and pamphlet distribution. These media can be used effectively either individually or in a combination. The major difference between the methods such as telemarketing, catalog marketing, etc. is that in telemarketing and catalog marketing, the customer can be addressed individually, while this is difficult with newspapers, magazines, journals, and such other media. The usage of such media should be carefully planned, depending on the response patterns of the target customers. Some customer may respond quickly to catalog, while some prefer to respond to company newsletter. Magazine meant for investors or managers of small companies or industry-related magazine will get a good response only from readers of these magazines. On the other hand general magazines related to sports or entertainment is not targeted to specific type of customers. Through the target audiences will be wide; the response rate will be lower.

Some promotional materials, like coupons in magazine, usually get a better response from customers. Newspaper and magazines inserts also have a considerable advantage as a marketer has freedom with respect to the design, color, type, of paper, etc. in comparison with a newspaper advertisement.

These days, mobile phones are becoming a big attraction for marketers to promote their products. Telemarketing is highly efficient because it is targeted, personal and conducive to response. Sales efforts are focused on those people who are most likely to respond. It is not used for cold calling but more often to follow-up on leads generated by mails or print advertisement as well as to sell additional product to existing customers. Though immediate sales may not materialise on the phone, but once a comprehensive list is drawn up, telemarketing helps in grading purchase intentions, persuading the reluctant, weeding out the uninterested and following up productive enquires promptly. Thus telemarketing is a dynamic medium which, when integrated into the total marketing process, will increase sales efficiency and profits and above all maintain contact with the most priceless assets the customer.

Personal selling take s place when a seller or salesperson, do a face-to-face interaction with a potential customer, and tries to persuade him to buy the product or service he is promoting on behalf of the company. It takes place at a personal level and involves a personalised transaction. It provides the salesperson the immediate feedback and helps him adjust or modify his sales prepositions to suit the requirements of the customer.

Q4. What is Direct mail, its objective and its techniques?

Ans. The technology has become the predominant elements in many businesses. Information Technology has added to the capabilities of companies enabling them set new standards in business. The power of internet has transformed everything. E-commerce has redefine markets, industries and the way one does business. The growth of direct mail or direct response marketing has just begun and it is at an early stage of evolution.

The advantages associated with it are as follows:-
- It can reach a large customer base. In fact, marketing can be done on global basis using the internet and it enables marketers to potential customer around the world.
- It allows customer to shop online at their convenience from their home or workplace, and provide them statistics and video clips, also ample scope to compare products and services with of the competitors
- There is a direct interaction between marketers and the customer. Thus both buyer and seller have a close relationship.

The four primary objective of an effective direct mail campaign are:-

- It can be used to introduce sales people, promote other forms of advertising or announce a product introduction and for generating sales.
- It can be effectively used to build long-term customer relationship.
- Direct mail can alert dealers to future customer promotions, educate them on service problems and survey them concerning their needs.
- It can also be used to build company morale.

Wondering who is Gullybaba?

Gullybaba is a combination of two significant words **'Gully'** & **'Baba'**. The word 'Gully' comes from the ancient game played in Rural India–**Tip cat**. In Hindi, we call it **Gully Danda (गुल्ली डंडा)** which is a great **symbol of Focus & Fitness**.

The word 'Baba' stands for **Respect & Honour**. And these are the fundamental parameters for achieving success. **Focus & Fitness** are required to help one go a long way in life. This is all about achieving excellence in education and giving respect & honour to everyone, and thus, the name 'Gullybaba'.

To know more about why name GullyBaba visit: **GullyBaba.com/why-name-gullybaba.html**

Chapter-14

Publicity and Public Relations

Q1. What do you mean by public relation and what is its scope?

Ans. A firm's public includes its employees, stakeholders, trade unions, general public, customer, charities, media, government and politicians, etc. An organisation needs to communicate with the public both internally as well as externally. As the attitude of the public influences the sales of an organisation, enhanced public relations work to enhance the overall image and create goodwill for the company. Hence, organisation needs to communicate with one or all members of its public regularly.

The role of public relation is to; identify the relevant public, influence the opinion of the public by; reinforcing the favorable opinions, transforming neutral opinions of the public into positive opinions, changing or neutralising hostile opinions.

Publicity, is function of public relation in which communication is been done about an organisation or its product to the public. It is usually carried out in the form of; news item, a press release, or an article in a newspaper or through a mass medium like television, an interview or speech delivered by the executive of the company at a press conference, or one-to-one communication with the target audience. Public relation department was considered to be small attachment to a large corporation with four major functional areas; Finance, Operation, Marketing, and Human Resource Management. It is a department which works as a bridge between various publics of the organisation and the various functional departments.

Q2. What is the objectives of PR?

Ans. The objectives of PR are as follows:-

- At the time of new product launched or existing product relaunching, it can be used to generate the attention of the customer and the awareness through special events.
- It can help in creating interest or can influence the targeted customer to purchase the product.
- It can be used to provide in depth information about product and services. Through articles, collateral materials, newsletters and websites, PR delivers information to customers that can help them gain understanding of the product.
- A positive article in a newspaper, on a TV news show or mentioned on the Internet, often results in a discernable increase in product sales.
- In many companies the public relations function is also involved with brand reinforcement by maintaining positive relationships with key audiences, and thereby aiding in building a strong image. Today it is ever more important for companies and brands to build a good image. A strong image helps the company build its business and it can help the company in times of crises as well.

Q3. How public relation helps in marketing?

Ans. In a complex and hugely competitive market place, marketing and the disciplines within it must work seamlessly together. Marketing and public relations need one another--a good reputation makes marketing something easier, while effective marketing means the PR function has a real "hook" on which to base itself--but they work differently. Specific target markets and goals drive marketing, while PR focuses on creating a "buzz" or positive feeling around a specific entity or product

PR, whether proactive or reactive, boosts an organisation's profile in a positive way. Proactive PR might involve placing editorials in industry publications, arranging for a key figure to deliver a press conference on a new development or finding a celebrity to endorse a product. Reactive PR includes coordinating a response to a negative press story (also known as damage control), providing editorials to journalists and media evaluation.

Marketing usually serves as the umbrella under which the other communications disciplines sit. Marketing targets specific audiences, aiming to make them purchase a product, click through an email to visit a website or use a coupon. It serves as a means to retain customers by regular contact that builds and maintains a relationship, such as by personalised emails or direct mail.

❑❑❑

Chapter-15

Social Marketing Communication

Q1. Write down the process of communication plan.
Ans. The entire communication plan follows a sequence of 5 steps known as the planning cycle. It is a continuous cycle of events' and activities, which not only provide a plan focus, but also ensure that feedback and monitoring, improve the quality of communication effect.

Steps 1 & 2 Situation Analysis: The first two steps comprise the Situation Analysis in any communication program. An understanding of the current state of problems, and of the program that is in place to tackle it, gives us the answer to the first question. Answering the second question involves an assessment of the affected groups of people, how they have responded to past efforts at communication, identification of groups that continue to influence their behavior, and if all media channels are being used effectively to reach the target groups. It allows us to identify those factors in problem improvement that can be addressed through communication, and those that require programmatic intervention. Research plays an important role in identifying behavioral motives and media habits at this stage.

Step 3: Setting Objectives: The next step is to identify the specific role that communication should play in addressing the problems identified, and whether the emphasis should be on changing behavior, attitudes or just increasing the knowledge levels. It is often useful to include some supplementary objectives in terms of wider social issues such as gender, and disabilities, so that they may be reflected in the communication that is finally produced. Setting objectives allows you to be accountable for the work that you do - because in the development sector, success is measured not in terms of the revenues or profits that you make, but in terms of the number of people whose attitudes and behavior you have changed.

Step 4: Strategic Plan and Creative Approaches: In answering the question 'How do we get there?' you will choose the most effective strategy for the communication program, and 'develop a creative route and choose or devise appropriate media vehicles to reach the various audiences. This in essence will be the Communication Plan, which will detail the messages and media for each target group.

Step 5: Monitoring and Evaluation: This last step is an assessment of the effect of the communication, and ensures that the plan is implemented well. It will help you identify bottlenecks and give valuable pointers as to what to do the next time around.

Q2. What is the objective of communication?

Ans. Communication is the process of sending and receiving messages. However it is said to be effective only when the message is understood and when it stimulates action or encourages the receiver to think in new ways. It can do the following things: Increase awareness, encourage trail, provide information, build self reliance, change attitude, change behavior, reinforce behavior, and support delivery. Once you got down the list of what communication can do, the next step is prioritisation of the things.

Communication use SMART work objective in which, SMART stands for

- **Specific:** Is it clear and well defined, Is it clear to anyone that has a basic knowledge of the work area.
- **Measurable:** Know if the goal is obtainable and how far away completion is, Know when it has been achieved.
- **Achievable:** Agreement with all the stakeholders what the goals should be, Is there a realistic path to achievement.
- **Realistic:** Within the availability of resources, knowledge and time.
- **Timely:** Enough time to achieve the goal, is there a time limit, Not too much time, which can affect work performance.

Chapter-16

Functions and Structure of Ad Agency

Q1. What is the role of advertising agency?
Ans. A company can handle an adverting campaign on its own or it can hire the services of an advertising agency. But the advertising job has become so complex that almost all business prefer to engage advertising agencies. An advertising agency is a firm, which specialises in developing and running advertising campaigns through various media. They usually charge a percentage of the total cost of running a campaign as a commission for their services.

A small firm depends on smaller agencies or local newspapers and broadcasting stations to develop its artwork and in media scheduling, whereas some large firms have an advertising departments with in-house copywriters, artists, legal advisors, media personnel etc. These firms can either opt to develop their own campaign or hire the services of advertising agencies, depending on their specific needs. The advertising agency and its client (company) develop the advertising campaign jointly, the contribution of each party depends on the working relationship between them.

Q2. What is the function and structure of an advertising agency?
Ans. There are SIX major departments in any advertising agency. These can be split into other sub-departments, or given various creative names, but the skeleton is the same. These departments are:

(1) **Account Services:** The account service department comprises account executives, account managers and account directors, and is responsible for liaising with the agency's many clients. This

department is the link between the many departments within the agency, and the clients who pay the bills. In the past they were referred to as "the suits," and there have been many battles between the account services department and the creative department. But as most creative know, a good account services team is essential to a good advertising campaign. A solid creative brief is one of the main duties of account services.

(2) **Account Planning**: This department combines research with strategic thinking. Often a mix of researchers and account managers, the account planning department provides consumer insights, strategic direction, research, focus groups and assists helps keep advertising campaigns on target and on brand. To be truly effective, advertising must be both distinctive and relevant, and planning helps on both counts."

(3) **Creative**: This is the engine of any advertising agency. It's the lifeblood of the business, because the creative department is responsible for the product. And an ad agency is only as good as the ads the creative department puts out. The roles within the creative department are many and varied, and usually include:

- Copywriters,
- Art Directors,
- Designers,
- Production Artists,
- Web Designers,
- Associate Creative Directors,
- Creative Director(s).

In many agencies, copywriters and art directors are paired up, working as teams. They will also bring in the talents of other designers and production artists as and when the job requires it. Sometimes, traffic is handled by a position within the creative department, although that is usually part of the production department. Everyone within creative services reports to the Creative Director. It is his or her role to steer the creative product, making sure it is on brand, on brief and on time.

(4) **Finance & Accounts**: Money. At the end of the day, that's what ad agencies want. And it's what their clients want, too. At the center of all the money coming into, and going out of, the agency is the finance and accounts department. This department is responsible for handling payment of salaries, benefits, vendor costs, travel, day-to-day business costs and everything else you'd expect from doing business. It's been said that approximately 70% of an ad agency's income pays salary and benefits

to employees. However, this figure varies depending on the sise and success of the agency in question.

(5) Media Buying: It is the function of the media buying department to procure the advertising time and/or space required for a successful advertising campaign. This includes TV and radio time, outdoor (billboards, posters, guerrilla), magazine and newspaper insertions, internet banners and takeovers, and, well, anywhere else an ad can be placed for a fee. This usually involves close collaboration with the creative department who came up with the initial ideas, as well as the client and the kind of exposure they want. This department is usually steered by a media director.

(6) Production: Ideas are just ideas until they're made real. This is the job of the production department. During the creative process, the production department will be consulted to talk about the feasibility of executing certain ideas. Once the ad is sold to the client, the creative and account teams will collaborate with production to get the campaign produced on budget. This can be anything from getting original photography or illustration produced, working with printers, hiring typographers and TV directors, and a myriad of other disciplines needed to get an ad campaign published. Production also works closely with the media department, who will supply the specs and deadlines for the jobs.

In small to mid-sised agencies, traffic is also a part of the production department. It is the job of traffic to get each and every job through the various stages of account management, creative development, media buying and production in a set timeframe. Traffic will also ensure that work flows through the agency smoothly, preventing jams that may overwhelm creative teams and lead to very long hours, missed deadlines and problematic client relationships. Traffic keeps the agency's heart beating.

Larger agencies may also separate out the following departments:
- Human Resources & Facilities,
- Research,
- Web development,
- Traffic.

Q3. Before preparing the advertisement firms must take care of product and market. Explain.

Ans. It is very important for any advertising company before starting upon advertising making; it should devote some time on understanding the product and market. For whom it is going to work for.

(1) The Industry
- **Companies in industry:** total sales, strength, etc.
- **Growth patterns within industry:** primary demand curve, per capita consumption, growth potential.
- **History of industry:** technological ' advance trends etc.
- **Characteristics of industry:** distribution patterns, industry control, -promotional activity, geographic--characteristics, profit patterns, etc.

(2) The Company: The company story: history, sise, growth, profitability, scope of business, competence in various areas, reputation, strengths, weaknesses, etc.

(3) The Product or Service: The product story: development, quality, design, description, packaging, price structure, uses (primary, secondary, potential), reputation, strengths, weaknesses etc.
- Product sales features: exclusive, non-exclusive differentiating qualities, product's competitive position in mind of consumer, etc.
- Product research: improvements planned.

(4) Sales history: Sales and sales costs by product, model, sales districts, etc., Profit history.

(5) Share of market:
- **Sales history industry wide** share of market in rupees and units.
- **Market potential:** industry trends, company trends, demand trends.

(6) The Market: Who and where is market, how has market been segmented in the past, how can it be segmented in future, what are consumer needs, attitudes, and characteristics? How, why, when, and where do consumers buy ?
- Past advertising appeals which have proved successful or unsuccessful in speaking to consumer needs.
- Who are our customers, past customers, future customers? What characteristics do they have in common? What do they like about our product?, What don't they like ?

(7) Distribution: - History and evaluation of how and where product is distributed, current trend.
- Company's relationship with and attitudes of members of the distribution\ channel toward product/company.
- Past policies regarding trade advertising, deals, co-op advertising programms, etc.
- Status of trade literature, dealer promotions, point-of-purchase, displays, etc.

(8) Pricing policies: Price history: trends, relationship to needs of buyers, competitive price situation,
- Past price objectives: management attitudes, buyer attitudes, channel attitudes, etc.

(9) Competition: With Whom competition is ? What is competition's growth history and sise?
- Strengths of competition: sales features, product quality, sise, etc. Weaknesses of competition.
- Marketing activities of competition: advertising promotions, distribution, sales force, etc. Estimated budget.

(10) Promotion: Successes and failures of past promotion policy, sales force, advertising publicity.
- Promotion expenditures: history, budget emphasis, relation to 'competition, trend.
- Advertising programmes: strategies, themes, campaigns.
- Sales force: sise, scope, ability, cost/sale.

Q4. What are the major decision areas in advertising?

Ans. Following are the major areas in which advertising has to take care before start advertising:
- **Setting advertising objectives:** When clients and agencies advertise to "keep their brand presence in the market" or "to create brand goodwill" it is an unhealthy sign. It shows a failure to define precise advertising objectives. When defining advertising objective, the management should be clear about what it seeks to achieve out of the year's advertising campaign and even out of specific advertisements.
- **Where and how often to spend the budget:** For Media planning, the first clue is given by the target audiences' media habits. The product itself is an important factor in choosing the media. New

products whose usage has to be explained are best shown by demonstration.

- **When to spend:** The phasing of advertising is also a decision to be taken by the agency.

  In (i) the advertising expenditure is kept constant throughout irrespective of the cyclical nature or seasonality. This helps keep consumer awareness alive even in the sales through. Alternative (ii) is an innovative alternative when maximum advertising is done during the lowest sales period. This approach may be useful in making consumer demand less cyclical in the long run. This approach may not apply, to seasonal products (iii) is found to be quite popular among advertisers. Through it gives advertisers return for the advertising rupee in the short run, no long term thinking to steady the demand pattern is made. Alternative (iv) is based on the thinking that' a minimum threshold level of advertising should be maintained throughout the year. This helps in making demand non cyclical in the long run. The thrust of advertising is made just before the demand begins to look up.

  The assumption is that this is the time when potential consumers begin to think about the product purchase. Advertising at this time would have the maximum impact because rate of growth of demand is to be the highest. When rates of growth of demand drop advertising is also curtailed. Since there is a time-lag between advertising and sales hence advertising peak comes before the sales peak.

  Deciding What to Say': A critical decision facing the account executive in the agency and the client is to judge the output of agency's creative after a marketing advertising brief have resulted in the creative brief given to the agency's creative department.

While designing and evaluating the creative strategy the agency should keep the following checkpoints in the mind:-

- **Make the Creative Strategy fit the Marketing Plan:-** All the 4Ps of Marketing should be in harmony. Advertising should not take off in a different direction that one than the product, price and packaging are going.
- **Keep your objectives reasonable:** -Take the case of iced tea. The Indian consumer was in no mood to change his habits or take the

case of a company who tried to give canned food over a decade ago when the proportion . of working women was not so large and the joint family system was still prevalent. The Indian customer refused to change his habit. A good campaign should address itself to a specified target audience and not to everybody. Over ambition destroys a good campaign. Similarly don't try to sell a product for all occasions. Attempting to change people's habits is not advisable. Asking people to change their brand is simpler.

- **Make your strategy easy to use:** The strategy should be as clearly defined as possible. It should not leave any room for misunderstanding. It should be precise and crisp and yet should give an idea of the backup rationale.
- **Be Single minded:** In best ideas are usually simple. This comes from giving the copywriter a good single-minded proposition about the product.
- **State a business Objective:** Help the customer focus in on what action he should take after hearing your message. Do you want the consumer to increase product usage? A good example is increasing the product usage of a shampoo from the hair to the full body. Another objective could be widening the market. The latest television advertisements of a popular shampoo show its usage for school going girls increasing the sise of the target audience for shampoos.
- **Decide where your business is going to come from:** This implies not only understanding who your target audience is but also understanding from which other products market can you steal your share. This is especially so when your product is no longer new and needs to bring new consumers in the market for its growth.
- **Understand your target audience:** A good campaign goes beyond product attribute to understanding the customer. A study of consumer attitudes and usage patterns helps the copywriter talk directly to the target audience.
- **Make a meaningful promise:** For advertising to do its job, the products benefit or promise to the customer must be strong and meaningful.

- **Support your promise:** Making a promise alone is not sufficient. Support the promise preferable with evidence or demonstration. Billions of dollars and millions of rupees have been spent advertising six adjectives: white, cool, power, refreshing, relief. But why should the consumer believe you?
- **Set yourself apart:** A critical element to success is the ability to find a vacant niche in the market. Avoid a positioning which is exactly the same as your competitors. If your product is in the same general area as the competition, build in some element that will set your brand apart. Positioning can be done on many variables.
- **Give your product a distinctive personality:** This is hard to do. It implies giving your product a personality that goes beyond the product itself, its an aura that helps set the brand apart from others.
- **Advertise what's important, not what's obvious:** Its obvious what Milkmaid is. But its not so obvious' what it can do. Hence the campaign of Milkmaid informs you about what all Milkmaid can do for you.
- **Think ahead:** Try and be first with a product.
- **Keep your strategy up-to-date:** Realise that the world is changing. Analyse your product and its positioning and see where it's open for attack.
- **Don't change your strategy without good reason:** Taking a hard look at the all parts of the business is essential before changing the strategy.
- **Put the strategy in writing:** IA written strategy will guide you when you fall in love with a campaign which is creative but doesn't position the product where you wanted it to be positioned. The first question to be asked of any advertisement is "Is it on strategy ?
- **Have a better product:** This is actually the first point.: But it's been placed here to highlight that a better product almost always wins in the end.

Determining Advertising Effectiveness: If all the marketing tasks have been executed as planned, the sales graph after a time lag is the best determinant of advertising effectiveness. To measure advertising effectiveness in the short run, say immediately after the campaign, we need to go back to our advertising objectives. Well defined advertising objectives make the research objectives easy to formulate. The concepts of market research apply to advertising research and need not be repeated here. Memory tests are frequently used in advertising research. Memory tests are broken into two categories: those stressing recognition and those stressing recall.

❑❑❑

Chapter-17

Managing Client Agency Relationship

Q1. What are the components of marketing mix in advertising agencies?

Ans. Service differs from goods in that they have certain unique characteristics such as intangibility, perishability, inseparability, and heterogeneity. These characteristics make it necessary to differentiate the marketing mix for services from the one for goods. The marketing mix for services is an extension of the marketing mix for products and goods, as a few more elements are added. In additional to the 4P's (product, price, place, & promotion) That comprise the traditional marketing mix for product & goods, the marketing mix for service consists of 3 more elements, namely, people, physical evidence, and process, to cater to the unique needs of service marketing. Thus the marketing mix consists of 7 P's.

- **People:** The term people refer to all those persons who are involved in the production and consumption of a service. They include the front-line employee of a service organisation and the customer purchasing the service. In service marketing customer becomes a part of the service delivery process due to the inseparability of service production from its consumption. Unlike product marketing, where customers passively consume the product, they play an active role in service marketing right from generation to consumption of the service. The customer of the company as well as those of competitors plays a role in the marketing of service, because there is a lot of scope for customer to influence one another through word-of-mouth publicity. The achievements of marketing goals in service organisation, therefore, depend largely on the human element involved.

- **Physical Evidence:** The intangibility element associated with services makes difficult for customers to evaluate the quality of a service. Hence marketers in service organisation in their attempts to offer something tangible, provide the customer physical evidence of the service offered. Physical evidence include tangible accompaniments to the service like the uniform worn by the staff of the service organisation, the ambiance in the lobby of a hotel, reports and brochures, business cards etc. By creating tangible attributes of something as intangible as service, service organisation facilitate customer evaluation of the service quality, and create a service experience.

- **Process:** Process management in service is essential to ensure consistent quality of service delivery. Process involves transforming a certain input into the desired output. It is the process of delivery that differentiates one service firm from another. The efficiency with which the service delivery process is executed determines the quality of the service. The quality of service will in turn determine its value and customer satisfaction. Thus in order to ensure customer satisfaction, service organisation must ensure that right steps are taken in the right direction and that right tools and techniques are used at the right time, so that the customer enjoys a unique service experience.

Q2. What is minimal marketing, hard sell marketing, and professional marketing, explain?

Ans. As with marketing of any business firm, there are three objectives that professional firms also seek: Sufficient demand, sustained growth and profitable volume. To achieve these objectives professional firms need to market them. The three styles of marketing for an agency (as for any professional firm) can be: minimal, hard-sell and professional marketing:

- **Minimal Marketing:** Minimal marketing is practiced by many firms offering professional services. These firms dislike thinking of themselves as businessmen, instead state that they are motivated by service. They think of marketing as a salesman's job and look down on business solicitation. They believe that their good work will get more clients.

- **Hard Sell Marketing:** Hard sell marketing is at the opposite end of the spectrum to minimal marketing. It reflects a total sales orientation, offering price discounts, bad mouthing competition, offering referral commissions and indulging in practices bordering on violating. professional codes of ethics. This approach forgets like any sales oriented approach, that there is more to business than attracting clients. Marketing involves a discipline of identifying and cultivating a market, choosing targets, developing services, formulating plans etc.
- **Professional Marketing:** This approach to marketing of professional services is in consonance with the professional code of ethics. Such an approach involves planning for long-range marketing objectives and works out strategies to match, training staff to improve the efficiency and effectiveness of marketing and personal selling, allocating time and budget to support marketing activity, ensuring that quality of professional services offered currently does not suffer as marketing activity is increased.

Such effort is usually preceded by gathering data about the market. Strategies are evolved thereafter. These strategies may include "service" or "market" specialisation. Specialisation in any particular service/range of services may give an agency a cutting edge with clients who are looking for those services. Similarly specialising in certain type of markets (say "public issues" market) may pre-empt segments of the market to the agency. Another strategy may be of expanding services to current clients.

Q3. What do you mean by positioning and what are the strategies for advertising agency?

Ans. Positioning can be defined as an activity of creating a brand offer in such a manner that it occupies a distinctive place and value in the target customer's mind. Positioning involves identifying and determining points of similarity and difference to ascertain the right brand identity and to create a proper brand image. Positioning is the key of marketing strategy. A strong brand positioning directs marketing strategy by explaining the brand details, the uniqueness of brand and it's similarity with the competitive brands, as well as the reasons for buying and using that specific brand. Positioning is the base for developing and increasing the required knowledge and perceptions of the customers. It is the single feature that sets your service apart from your competitors.

Positioning is the very important aspect of marketing a product or a service. The three broad positioning alternatives are product differentiation, as a low cost reader or as a reader. The firm should concentrate on one single strategy and excel in that rather than trying to be good at everything. These broad frameworks provide the firm with the basic foundation on which to build their positioning. Firms should look at strategies for specific positioning. These specific positioning strategies can be based on an attribute or benefit of the service to the consumer or competitor of the service. Some of these specific strategies are as follows:-

- **Attribute positioning:** A service provider position itself on an attribute or a feature. For example Times of India position itself as the number one daily in India with the most number of readers and Allahabad bank positions itself as the oldest bank in India. However positioning based on a feature or an attribute may not work too well for some service.
- **Benefit positioning:** Most service provider resort to benefit positioning as the general psyche of the customer is to analyse the benefit that he derives by using a particular service. For example, banks like ICICI and Citibank offer facilities like ATM's and internet banking to their customer.
- **Use/application positioning:** The service is positioned as the best for a certain application. For example, SBI positions itself as the best in the business where educational loans are concerned.
- **Competitor positioning:** The service is positioned by the provider against a competitors' service. For example IIPM position itself against the IIM's its advertisement says, "Dare to think beyond IIMs"
- **Category positioning:** The service provider positions itself as the category leader and becomes synonymous with the service. For example Essel word became synonymous with an entertainment park in India till more such parks are started across the country.
- **Quality/price positioning:** A service is positioned in the market as possessing a certain quality standard or at a particular price. For example, some of the Taj group is trying to position some of its hotel in the 'value for money' category.

Companies however, have to be careful in designing their positioning strategies and avoid some of the associated pitfalls. Some brands are under positioned when they try fail to provide a strong benefits or reason for the customer to choose them. On the other hand, some brands are over-positioned for a very narrow segment and so many potential customers fail to notice it. When a brand communicates two or more contradicting features/benefits, it is termed confused positioning. Irrelevant positioning is when the brand fails to attract any customer because of offering irrelevant and redundant features/benefits. It is termed doubtful positioning when a company promises something and the customer doubts its capacity or the brands capacity.

Q4. How do strategies vary according to the type of client and the agency sise?

Ans. If the agency sise is small, medium, or large it has select its client on basis of their capability to handle them if the agency take the large sise client and it is having small team how it can handle all the activities on time and can fail in the positioning of the client brand as well as its own image in the market. To understand, at what agency sise who is the right client is can be understand with help of the following strategy option:-

- **The Small Sise Agency:** Small agencies by their sise usually do not have very large brands to work on. The agency focus then largely becomes entrepreneurial, where the agency should have an ability to select clients whose products have a USP which is capable of becoming a benefit, highly desirable to a particular target audience in the market. At this stage, agency strategy involves a search for the right clients i.e. the agency should catch the entrepreneur who has a good product. The success of the brand then becomes the success of the agency. However, faulty selection and non-payment by the client is a risk. Hence mortality rate of small agencies is higher than for medium and large scale agencies. The other alternative strategy for a small sise agency could be to offer some specialised services. Clients, irrespective of sise, needing strengths in certain service areas would find such agencies useful. For example, agencies having good studio facilities could cater to clients who have needs of printing or other work requiring high quality artwork. In case a small agency has a large brand, its revenues become largely dependent on the brand. This is both a constraint and an opportunity. The constraint is that the brand portfolio of the agency is very narrow. Hence the agency could become over dependent on the brand. Such dependence may hamper giving professional advice, especially when it is unpleasant for the client. The opportunity is that the success of the brand is the key of the agency's success. If the agency realises this fully and establishes a healthy professional working relationship with the client it could be mutually very beneficial. The agency would devote its fullest energies to the success of the brand, giving a growing brand the attention it deserves. In the long run, it would be advisable for the agency to diversify its client mix, for recessionary market conditions in the agency's major brands market and subsequent financial involvement would be unmanageable for a small agency.

- **Medium Sise Agencies:** A medium sise agency should invest in tomorrow with small brands that it builds into leaders. It should have a balanced client mix. With more than a couple of brand leaders bringing the front, half a dozen or more, major brand players in their market and handful of small clients who have a potential for becoming leaders tomorrow. The advantage of the medium sise agency is clear. It is neither too big to be unaffected by a change in any client's health nor is it too small to avoid offering comprehensive advertising services. Its product portfolio, should consist of "today's bread winners" who are some large brands as well as "tomorrows bread winners" which are small brands the agency is nurturing to become brand leaders. The key benefit a medium sise agency offers its clients (its positioning statement) is that it is not too big for its clients to lack personalised agency attention. Neither is it too small to avoid investing in full fledged infrastructural support services. Therefore it can claim to offer the best of both worlds to a client.

- **Large sise agencies:** A large agency must heighten its positioning as a leader. This can be done by setting industry standards. A leading agency, for example, produced an Urban Market Index and Rural Market Index which not only helps other agencies but also clients in their planning. Another strategy is to help in creating better training facilities to train professionals for advertising. This creates goodwill as many students may move to client organisations. It also helps to attract the best talent, hence preserving the preeminent place for the agency in the long run. This could also he clone through organising seminars for both agencies and clients. Yet another strategy could be to create industry standards in auxiliary services like market research by setting up independent companies to handle these services. Such services can be used by both clients, and other agencies. The basic strategy is to help improve the quality of inputs for the advertising profession. The leading brands naturally choose the largest agencies. Hence a large agency's client list reads like a who's who of brands. The advantages of such a scenario are obvious. The disadvantages need looking at. Due to the sise of such agencies, it becomes unviable to handle brands who generate turnovers below a certain sise. This leads the "innovator entrepreneurs" who are creating new product categories and attacking new markets to look elsewhere. It therefore makes eminent sense for large agencies to set up smaller "slater" agencies who can not only handle such clients but can also pick up competitive brands to the parent agency's brands. The latter is identical to a "multi branding" strategy used by dominant companies to maximise market share in large markets. The launch strategy for these "sister" agencies could well be a positioning stance that is the antithesis to the larger parent agency. If the larger agency is perceived as one following classical rules of advertising, "the sister agency could well he a maverick". This would get both type of clients and brands and diversify the product/client mix of the group. Such an antithesis positioning would be useful when a larger growing segment of brands have a potential of succeeding using such a positioning stance. Usually the antithesis positioning of the smaller agency is "better servicing", "more time for client" etc. The positioning also reflects itself in clients chosen: they could he smaller say retail v/s manufacturers etc.

Chapter-18

Strategies for Account Management

Q1. What is a relation between communication & strategy?

Ans. Communication strategies are common in the business world, where they are used as part of a business' plan, detailing how to communicate with various groups of people. A single business may have multiple strategies for different categories of people, such as clients, investors, competitors, or employees. Some companies even have an internal communication strategy for communicating within the business itself. These strategies are used to determine things like what information to share with the clients or investors, as well as how that information should be presented. Communication and strategy building have moved so close to each other that it may now be difficult to understand one without appreciating the other. Communication and information technology have made the world a small place, simplified tedious tasks, increased consumer options, made information so easy to access that delivery of products and services can be revolutionised. Planning, communication and strategy building emerge as an integrated process in determining a firm's competitive response.

Planning and communication processes within a firm run parallel to each other. This enables the firm to continuously update itself with the growth in knowledge and use this knowledge to devise its own competitive strategy. In the last few decades growth of knowledge has had a tremendous impact on the efficacy of communication methods. Technology is continuously making communication simpler.

Growth of knowledge depends on the availability of information. Information needs to he sourced. This requires co-operation with those who possess it and building channels for its inward flow. The firms planning process increasingly depends on the ability to process this information with discrimination. The firms output or response to this inflow and its processing can be called as the firms competitive response.

The Planning Process and Communication Tasks have a parallel flow:

- **Inflow:** Information from many sources is available to a firm How to choose, the right sources that can help the value addition process of the firm is the first task. These sources could generally be suppliers, related industries, scientific community, new customers, present customers, trade association etc.
- **Processing:** The firm needs to evolve a discrimination process that first sifts the clutter from the information flow. Next it needs to build with its human capital the systems, processes, skills etc that can process this information inflow in a manner that can identify where value addition can be done by the firm. The nature of internal processes of the firm is important here.
- **Value added outflow:** Finally the firm needs to deliver value added to both customers and society. If the firms outflow also helps build value added for its suppliers or related industries, or even its competitors it can start a mutually supportive process of value addition helping create competitive advantage for the nation.

The growth of knowledge and the ability to translate it into value for customer depends on three things. Which are as follows:-

- **Cooperation:** The ability to find sources of information and the ability to build channels for their inward flow.
- **The ability to process and flow with discrimination:** This requires an ability to focus on the small things that make big things possible. This focused Concern is the strength firms need to develop to enable them to respond adequately to competition
- **Competitive response:** The ability to give a response in the market place that can differentiate the firm from its competitors by the fact that it has added value for its customers and has been able to communicate this value added to them.

All the above factors depend on communication. The firm has to plan for the future. This implies analysing not only the nature of competition but also the influence of knowledge on it. It also requires a recognition of the growing dependence of both planning and strategy development on communication.

Q2. Is any inter-relation among the three (planning, communication & strategy)?

Ans. Planning and Strategy depend on communication: The three tasks of planning, communication and strategy formulation are interdependent. Communication, however, is the key tool they use. The role of communication within the firm nurtures and fosters the process of bottom-up planning. One of the advantages of such a process could be what Rise and Trout call "Bottom-up" marketing where one marketing tactic generates the necessary value to build a strategy around it. When the same bottomup communication happens in non-marketing departments along with an up gradation of skills, knowledge of techniques of production and understanding of customer needs it could lead to cost advantage, productivity increases or even innovation as in new product and process ideas. The advantages that "good communicator" organisations have are the ones crucial to attaining strategic positions and competitive advantage. Hence both strategy and planning depend upon communication.

Communication, too, should grow from planning and strategy: Communication that germinates from needs of planning and subsequent development of strategy enables the creation and delivery of additional value, lower cost or both.

Q3. What is diamond theory?

Ans. The Diamond model of Michael Porter for the Competitive Advantage of Nations offers a model that can help understand the competitive position of a nation in global competition. Porter is a famous Harvard business professor. According to Porter, a nation attains a competitive advantage if its firms are competitive. Firms become competitive through innovation. Innovation can include technical improvements to the product or to the production process.

Four attributes of a nation comprise Michael Porter's "Diamond" of national advantage. They are:

(1) Factor Conditions: Factor conditions refers to inputs used as factors of production – such as labour, land, natural resources, capital and infrastructure. Porter argues that a lack of resources often actually helps countries to become competitive (call it selected factor disadvantage). Abundance generates waste and scarcity generates an innovative mindset. Such countries are forced to innovate to overcome their problem of scarce resources.

(2) Demand Conditions: Michael Porter argues that a sophisticated domestic market is an important element to producing competitiveness. Firms that face a sophisticated domestic market are likely to sell superior products because the market demands high quality and a close proximity to such consumers enables the firm to better understand the needs and desires of the customers. If the nation's discriminating values spread to other countries, then the local firms will be competitive in the global market.

(3) Related and Supporting Industries:- Porter also argues that a set of strong related and supporting industries is important to the competitiveness of firms. This includes suppliers and related industries. This usually occurs at a regional level as opposed to a national level.

(4) Firm Strategy, Structure and Rivalry:

(i) Strategy:

Capital Markets: Domestic capital markets affect the strategy of firms. Some countriesï¿½ capital markets have a long-run outlook, while others have a short-run outlook. Industries vary in how long the long-run is. Countries with a short-run outlook (like the U.S.) will tend to be more competitive in industries where investment is short-term (like the computer industry). Countries with a long run outlook (like Switzerland) will tend to be more competitive in industries where investment is long term (like the pharmaceutical industry).

Individuals Career Choices: Individuals base their career decisions on opportunities and prestige. A country will be competitive in an industry whose key personnel hold positions that are considered prestigious.

(ii) Structure: Porter argues that the best management styles vary among industries. Some countries may be oriented toward a particular style of management. Those countries will tend to be more competitive in industries for which that style of management is suited.

(iii) Rivalry: Porter argues that intense competition spurs innovation. International competition is not as intense and motivating. With international competition, there are enough differences between companies and their environments to provide handy excuses to managers who were outperformed by their competitors.

Q4. What is BCG-Matrix?

Ans. It is known as Boston Consulting Group (BCG) Matrix which is a four celled matrix (a 2 * 2 matrix) developed by BCG, USA. It is the most renowned corporate portfolio analysis tool. It provides a graphic representation for an organisation to examine different businesses in its portfolio on the basis of their related market share and industry growth rates. It is a two dimensional analysis on management of SBU's (Strategic Business Units). In other words, it is a comparative analysis of business potential and the evaluation of environment.

According to this matrix, business could be classified as high or low according to their industry growth rate and relative market share.

Relative Market Share = SBU Sales this year leading competitors sales this year.

Market Growth Rate = Industry sales this year - Industry Sales last year.

The analysis requires that both measures be calculated for each SBU. The dimension of business strength, relative market share, will measure comparative advantage indicated by market dominance. The key theory underlying this is existence of an experience curve and that market share is achieved due to overall cost leadership.

BCG matrix has four cells, with the horizontal axis representing relative market share and the vertical axis denoting market growth rate. The mid-point of relative market share is set at 1.0. if all the SBU's are in same industry, the average growth rate of the industry is used. While, if all the SBU's are located in different industries, then the mid-point is set at the growth rate for the economy.

Resources are allocated to the business units according to their situation on the grid. The four cells of this matrix have been called as stars, cash cows, question marks and dogs. Each of these cells represents a particular type of business.

- **Stars:** Stars represent business units having large market share in a fast growing industry. They may generate cash but because of fast growing market, stars require huge investments to maintain their lead. Net cash flow is usually modest. SBU's located in this cell are attractive as they are located in a robust industry and these business units are highly competitive in the industry. If successful, a star will become a cash cow when the industry matures.

- **Cash Cows:** Cash Cows represents business units having a large market share in a mature, slow growing industry. Cash cows require little investment and generate cash that can be utilised for investment in other business units. These SBU's are the corporation's key source of cash, and are specifically the core business. They are the base of an organisation. These businesses usually follow stability strategies. When cash cows lose their appeal and move towards deterioration, then a retrenchment policy may be pursued.

- **Question Marks:** Question marks represent business units having low relative market share and located in a high growth industry. They require huge amount of cash to maintain or gain market share. They require attention to determine if the venture can be viable. Question marks are generally new goods and services which have a good commercial prospective. There is no specific strategy which can be adopted. If the firm thinks it has dominant market share, then it can adopt expansion strategy, else retrenchment strategy can be adopted. Most businesses start as question marks as the company tries to enter a high growth market in which there is already a market-share. If ignored, then question marks may become dogs, while if huge investment is made, then they have potential of becoming stars.

- **Dogs:** Dogs represent businesses having weak market shares in low-growth markets. They neither generate cash nor require huge amount of cash. Due to low market share, these business units face cost disadvantages. Generally retrenchment strategies are adopted because these firms can gain market share only at the expense of competitor's/rival firms. These business firms have weak market share because of high costs, poor quality, ineffective marketing, etc. Unless a dog has some other strategic aim, it should be liquidated if there is fewer prospects for it to gain market share. Number of dogs should be avoided and minimised in an organisation.

Limitations of BCG Matrix: The BCG Matrix produces a framework for allocating resources among different business units and makes it possible to compare many business units at a glance. But BCG Matrix is not free from limitations, such as:

- BCG matrix classifies businesses as low and high, but generally businesses can be medium also. Thus, the true nature of business may not be reflected.
- Market is not clearly defined in this model.
- High market share does not always leads to high profits. There are high costs also involved with high market share.
- Growth rate and relative market share are not the only indicators of profitability. This model ignores and overlooks other indicators of profitability.
- At times, dogs may help other businesses in gaining competitive advantage. They can earn even more than cash cows sometimes.
- This four-celled approach is considered as to be too simplistic.

Q5. What is Porters generic strategy?

Ans. Generic strategies were used initially in the early 1980s, by Michael porter and seem to be even more popular today. Porter suggested that businesses can secure a sustainable competitive advantage by adopting one of three generic strategies. A firm's relative position within its industry determines whether a firm's profitability is above or below the industry average. The fundamental basis of above average profitability in the long run is sustainable competitive advantage. There are two basic types of competitive advantage a firm can possess: low cost or differentiation. The two basic types of competitive advantage combined with the scope of activities for which a firm seeks to achieve them, lead to three generic strategies for achieving above average performance in an industry: cost leadership, differentiation, and focus. The focus strategy has two variants, cost focus and differentiation focus. He also identified a fourth strategy "middle of the road" strategy, which although adopted by some businesses, is unlikely to create a competitive advantage.

- **Cost Leadership:** The low cost leader in any market gains competitive advantage from being able to many to produce at the lowest cost. Factories are built and maintained; labor is recruited and trained to deliver the lowest possible costs of production. 'cost advantage' is the focus. Costs are shaved off every element of the value chain. Products tend to be 'no frills.' However, low cost does not always lead to low price. Producers could price at competitive parity, exploiting the benefits of a bigger margin than competitors. Some organisations, such as Toyota, are very good not only at producing high quality autos at a low price, but have the brand and marketing skills to use a premium pricing policy.

- **Differentiation:** Differentiated goods and services satisfy the needs of customers through a sustainable competitive advantage. This allows companies to desensitise prices and focus on value that generates a comparatively higher price and a better margin. The benefits of differentiation require producers to segment markets in order to target goods and services at specific segments, generating a higher than average price. For example, British Airways differentiates its service.

  The differentiating organisation will incur additional costs in creating their competitive advantage. These costs must be offset by the increase in revenue generated by sales. Costs must be recovered. There is also the chance that any differentiation could be copied by competitors. Therefore there is always an incentive to innovated and continuously improve.

- **Focus or Niche strategy:** The focus strategy is also known as a 'niche' strategy. Where an organisation can afford either a wide scope cost leadership or a wide scope differentiation strategy, a niche strategy could be more suitable. Here an organisation focuses effort and resources on a narrow, defined segment of a market. Competitive advantage is generated specifically for the niche. A niche strategy is often used by smaller firms. A company could use either a cost focus or a differentiation focus.

  With a cost focus a firm aims at being the lowest cost producer in that niche or segment. With a differentiation focus a firm creates competitive advantage through differentiation within the niche or segment. There are potentially problems with the niche approach. Small, specialist niches could disappear in the long term. Cost focus is unachievable with an industry depending upon economies of scale e.g. telecommunications

- **Stuck In The Middle:** Some businesses will attempt to adopt all three strategies; cost leadership, differentiation and niche (focus). A business adopting all three strategies is known as "stuck in the middle". They have no clear business strategy and are attempting to be everything to everyone. This is likely to increase running costs and cause confusion, as it is difficult to please all sectors of the market. Middle of the road businesses usually do the worst in their industry because they are not concentrating on one business strength.

Chapter-19

Legal and Ethical Issues in Advertising

Q1. What are legal provision given by the Indian Law for advertising?

Ans. At present in India, there is no central statutory agency or uniform legislation regulating the advertising industry. The Indian advertising market as a whole is regulated and controlled by a non-statutory body, the **Advertising Standards Council of India (ASCI)**. In the absence of uniform integrated legislation, it is necessary for advertisers to ensure that an advertisement is in compliance will all local and national advertisement laws. To work in an ethical environment one has to follow the rules and regulation made by the government. Some of the legal provisions are as follow:

(1) Advertising to Children (advertising during and immediately before and after children's programming): The Young Persons (Harmful Publications) Act, 1956 prohibits advertisements relating to any harmful publication i.e., any publication that tends to corrupt a young person (person under the age of 18 years) by inciting or encouraging him or her to commit offenses or acts of violence or cruelty or in any other manner whatsoever. According to the ASCI Code, advertisements addressed to minors shall not contain anything, whether in illustration or otherwise, which might result in their physical, mental, or moral harm or which exploits their vulnerability. For example, advertisements may not:

- Encourage minors to enter strange places or to converse with strangers in an effort to collect coupons, wrappers, labels or the like.

- Feature dangerous or hazardous acts which are likely to encourage minors to emulate such acts in a manner which could cause harm or injury.
- Show minors using or playing with matches or any inflammable or explosive substance; or playing with or using sharp knives, guns, or mechanical or electrical appliances, the careless use of which could lead to their suffering cuts, burns, shocks, or other injury.
- Feature minors in promoting tobacco or alcohol-based products.
- Feature personalities from the field of sports, music, or cinema for products which, by law, either require a health warning in their advertising or cannot be purchased by minors.

(2) Comparative Advertising (ads that compare the advertiser's product to that of a competitor): The provisions pertaining to comparative representation were part of "Unfair Trade Practice" under the Monopolies and Restrictive Trade Practices Act, 1969 (MRTP Act). After repeal of the MRTP Act, the provisions relating to unfair trade practices were inserted in the Consumer Protection Act, 1986. However, a business entity cannot claim relief against unfair comparative advertising under the Consumer Protection Act, as a business entity is not a consumer. This can be taken up only by consumer associations, the central government, or state governments, and it does not provide protection to the business entity equal to the protection under the MRTP Act. Thus, under the existing law, a manufacturer whose goods are disparaged has no standing to seek a remedy. Presently, in the absence of any specific legislative regulating comparative advertising, disputes are decided by various courts on the basis of the facts in each case. However, ASCI code (which is made part of the Cable Television Network Rules, 1994 as well) permits advertisement containing comparisons including those where a competitor is named in the interests of vigorous competition and public enlightenment, provided:

- It is clear what aspects of the advertiser's product are being compared with what aspects of the competitor's product.
- The subject matter of comparison is not chosen in such a way as to confer an artificial advantage upon the advertiser or so as to suggest that a better bargain is offered than is truly the case.
- The comparisons are factual, accurate and capable of substantiation.

- There is no likelihood of the consumer being misled as a result of the comparison, whether about the product advertised or that with which it is compared.
- The advertisement does not unfairly denigrate, attack or discredit other products, advertisers or advertisements directly or by implication.

Presently, ASCI is actively taking action against any advertisements making unsubstantiated claims, exaggeration, unfair denigration in violation of ASCI Code.

(3) Contests (games of chance and games of skill): The Public Gambling Act, 1867 prohibits gambling activities in India. However, the Public Gambling Act permits games of mere skill.

(4) Deceptive or Misleading Advertising: Deceptive or misleading advertisements are restricted under the various legislations including the Consumer Protection Act, 1986; Cable Television Network Rules, 1994; Norms for Journalist Conduct issued by the Press Council of India Act and ASCI Code.

(5) Surrogate Advertising: The ASCI code provides that advertisements of products whose advertising is prohibited or restricted by law or by the ASCI Code must not circumvent such restrictions by purporting to be advertisements for other products the advertising of which is not prohibited or restricted by law or by ASCI Code. To determine if there is an indirect advertisement of prohibited products due attention shall be given to the following:
- Visual content of the advertisement must depict only the product being advertised and not the prohibited or restricted product in any form or manner:
- The advertisement must not make any direct or indirect reference to the prohibited or restricted products
- The advertisement must not create any nuances or phrases promoting prohibited products
- The advertisement must not use particular colours and layout or presentations associated with prohibited or restricted products
- The advertisement must not use situations typical for promotion of prohibited or restricted products when advertising the other products.

The Cable Television Networks Rules, 1995 has also imposed similar restrictions to curb surrogate advertising.

(6) Advertorials and Disguised Ads: The Norms for Journalist Conduct issued by the Press Council of India, Cable Television Network Rules, 1994 and Advertising Code of Doordarshan requires that advertisements must be clearly distinguishable from news content carried in the newspaper.

(7) False Advertising: False advertisements are restricted under the various legislations including the Consumer Protection Act, 1986; Cable Television Network Rules, 1994; Norms for Journalist Conduct issued by the Press Council of India Act and ASCI Code.

(8) "Free" Gifts/Samples: The Consumer Protection Act 1986, Section 2 (3) (a) states that (i) the offering of gifts, prises or other items with the intention of not providing them as offered or creating impression that something is being given or offered free of charge when it is fully or partly covered by the amount charged in the transaction as a whole, or (ii) the conduct of any contest, lottery, game of chance or skill, for the purpose of promoting, directly or indirectly, the sale, use or supply of any product or any business interest, is an unfair trade practice.

The Norms for Journalist Conduct issued by the Press Council of India has stated that gift including those given by the advertisement agencies for publication of material relating to their clients or otherwise should not be accepted by the journalist.

(9) Free Speech (specific limitations, e.g. personal slurs, defamation, political statements): Article 19(1)(a) of the Constitution of India protects the right to freedom of speech and expression, which is also extended to advertisements. However, like any other right, this freedom is also subject to reasonable restrictions imposed by Article 19(2) of the Constitution of India.

The various Acts, which have to be taken into consideration when dealing with the regulations imposed upon the Print Media, are:

- **The Press and Registration of Books Act, 1867** – This Act regulates printing presses and newspapers and makes registration with an appointed Authority compulsory for all printing presses.
- **The Press (Objectionable Matters) Act, 1951** – This enactment provides against the printing and publication of incitement to crime and other objectionable matters.
- **The Newspaper (Prices and Pages) Act, 1956** – This statute empowers the Central Government to regulate the price of newspapers in relation to the number of pages and sise and also

to regulate the allocation of space to be allowed for advertising matter.

The various Acts, which have to be taken into consideration when dealing with the regulations imposed upon the Electronic Media, are:

(1) The Broadcasting Code, adopted by the Fourth Asian Broadcasting Conference in 1962 listing certain cardinal principles to be followed buy the electronic media, is of prime importance so far as laws governing broadcast medium are concerned. Although, the Broadcast Code was chiefly set up to govern the All India Radio, the following cardinal principles have ideally been practiced by all Broadcasting and Television Organisation; viz:

- To ensure the objective presentation of news and fair and unbiased comment.
- To promote the advancement of education and culture.
- To raise and maintain high standards of decency and decorum in all programmes.
- To promote communal harmony, religious tolerance and international understanding.
- To treat controversial public issues in an impartial and dispassionate manner.
- To respect human rights and dignity.

(2) Cable Television Networks (Regulation) Act, 1995 basically regulates the operation of Cable Television in the territory of India and regulates the subscription rates and the total number of total subscribers receiving programmes transmitted in the basic tier. In pursuance of the Cable Television Network (Regulation) (Amendment) Bill, 2002, the Central Government may make it obligatory for every cable operator to transmit or retransmit programme of any pay channel through an addressable system as and when the Central Government so notifies. Such notification may also specify the number of free to air channels to be included in the package of channels forming the basic service tier.

(3) Direct-to-Home Broadcasting: Direct-to-Home (DTH) Broadcasting Service, refers to distribution of multi-channel TV programmes in Ku Band by using a satellite system and by providing TV signals directly to the subscribers' premises without passing through an intermediary such as a cable operator. The Union Government has decided to permit Direct-to-Home TV service in Ku band in India.

Film: India is one of the largest producers of motion pictures in the world. Encompassing three major spheres of activity – production, distribution and exhibition, the industry has an all-India spread, employing thousands of people and entertaining millions each year. The various laws in force regulating the making and screening of films are: -

(1) The Cinematograph Act, 1952: The Cinematograph Act of 1952 has been passed to make provisions for a certification of cinematographed films for exhibitions by means of Cinematograph. Under this Act, a Board of Film Censors (now renamed Central Board of Film Certification) with advisory panels at regional centres is empowered to examine every film and sanction it whether for unrestricted exhibition or for exhibition restricted to adults. The Board is also empowered to refuse to sanction a film for public exhibition.

(2) The Copyright Act, 1957: According to this Act, 'copyright' means the exclusive right to commercially exploit the original literary, dramatic, artistic, musical work, sound recordings or cinematographic films as per the wishes of the owner of copyright subject to the restrictions imposed in the Act.

Although this Act is applicable to all the branches of media, in some areas it is specific to this particular genre. In the case of a Cinematographed film, to do or to authorise the doing of any of the following acts would lead to the infringement of copyright. Those acts are namely: -

- To make a copy of the film
- To cause the film, in so far, as it consists of visual images, to be seen in public and in so far as it consists of sounds to be heard in public.
- To make any record embodying the recording in any part of the soundtrack associated with the film by utilising such sound track.
- To communicate the film by radio-diffusion.

(3) Cine Workers and Cinema Theatre Workers (Regulation of Employment) Act, 1981: This legislation affords a measure of protection to those employed in the industry by imposing certain obligations on motion picture producers and theatre owners concerning the former's condition of service.

(4) Cine Workers Welfare Cess Act, 1981 and the Cine Workers Welfare Fund Act 1981: They seek to create means of financial support to cine employees, the seasonal and unpredictable nature of whose employment often leaves them impoverished and helpless. Besides these, there are also a few local legislations, which affect the film medium; viz.

(5) The Bombay Police Act, 1951: It contains provisions empowering the police to regulate the exhibition of films in the state of Maharashtra (formerly Bombay).

(6) Bombay Cinemas (Regulation) Act, 1953: It provides a scheme for state licensing of cinema theatres and other places where motion pictures are exhibited.

(7) The Bombay Entertainments Duty Act, 1923: It imposes a tax on the public exhibition of motion pictures and other forms of entertainment.

Q2. What is the importance of ethics in advertising?

Ans. Ethics means a set of moral principles which govern a person's behavior or how the activity is conducted. And advertising means a mode of communication between a seller and a buyer. Thus ethics in advertising means a set of well defined principles which govern the ways of communication taking place between the seller and the buyer. Ethics is the most important feature of the advertising industry. Though there are many benefits of advertising but then there are some points which don't match the ethical norms of advertising. An ethical ad is the one which doesn't lie, doesn't make fake or false claims and is in the limit of decency.

The main area of interest for advertisers is to increase their sales, gain more and more customers, and increase the demand for the product by presenting a well decorated, puffed and colorful ad They claim that their product is the best, having unique qualities than the competitors, more cost effective, and more beneficial. But most of these ads are found to be false, misleading customers and unethical. The best example of these types of ads is the one which shows evening snacks for the kids, they use coloring and gluing to make the product look glossy and attractive to the consumers who are watching the ads on television and convince them to buy the product without giving a second thought.

(1) Ethics in Advertising is directly related to the purpose of advertising and the nature of advertising. Sometimes exaggerating the ad becomes necessary to prove the benefit of the product. For e.g. a sanitary napkin ad which shows that when the napkin was dropped in a river by some girls, the napkin soaked whole water of the river. Thus, the purpose of advertising was only to inform women about the product quality. Obviously, every woman knows that this cannot practically happen but the ad was accepted. This doesn't show that the ad was unethical.

(2) Ethics also depends on what we believe. If the advertisers make the ads on the belief that the customers will understand, persuade them to think, and then act on their ads, then this will lead to positive results and the ad may not be called unethical. But at the same time, if advertisers believe that they can fool their customers by showing any impractical things like just clicking fingers will make your home or office fully furnished or just buying a lottery ticket will make you a millionaire, then this is not going to work out for them and will be called as unethical.

We should follow three moral principles while preparing advertisement – Truthfulness, Social Responsibility and Upholding Human Dignity.

Generally, big companies never lie as they have to prove their points to various ad regulating bodies. Truth is always said but not completely. Sometimes it's better not to reveal the whole truth in the ad but at times truth has to be shown for betterment.

- **Pharmaceutical Advertising:** they help creating awareness, but one catchy point here is that the advertisers show what the medicine can cure but never talk about the side effects of that same thing or the risks involved in intake of it.

- **Children:** children are the major sellers of the ads and the product. They have the power to convince the buyers. But when advertisers are using children in their ad, they should remember not to show them alone doing there work on their own like brushing teeth, playing with toys, or infants holding their own milk bottles as everyone knows that no one will leave their kids unattended while doing all these activities. So showing parents also involved in all activities or things being advertised will be more logical.

- **Alcohol:** till today, there hasn't come any liquor ad which shows anyone drinking the original liquor. They use mineral water and sodas in their advertisements with their brand name. These types of ads are called surrogate ads. These type of ads are totally unethical when liquor ads are totally banned. Even if there are no advertisements for alcohol, people will continue drinking.

- **Cigarettes and Tobacco:** these products should be never advertised as consumption of these things is directly and badly responsible for cancer and other severe health issues. These as are already banned in countries like India, Norway, Thailand, Finland and Singapore.

- **Ads for social causes:** these types of ads are ethical and are accepted by the people. But ads like condoms and contraceptive pills should be limited, as these are sometimes unethical, and are more likely to loose morality and decency at places where there is no educational knowledge about all these products.

Looking at all these above mentioned points, advertisers should start taking responsibility of self regulating their ads by:
- Design self regulatory codes in their companies including ethical norms, truth, decency, and legal points
- Keep tracking the activities and remove ads which don't fulfill the codes.
- Inform the consumers about the self regulatory codes of the company
- Pay attention on the complaints coming from consumers about the product ads.
- Maintain transparency throughout the company and system.
- When all the above points are implemented, they will result in:
- Making the company answerable for all its activities
- It will reduce the chances of getting pointed out by the critics or any regulatory body.
- It will help gain confidence of the customers, make them trust the company and their products.

Question Papers

Management of Marketing Communication and Advertising: MS-68
June, 2020

Note: (i) Answer any three questions from Section A. (ii) Section B is compulsory. (iii) All questions carry equal marks.

Section—A

Q1. (a) Discuss the communication model that describe how communication travels from the firm to the consumer and the factors that affect the way the consumers perceive the message.

(b) Why do firms advertise? Explain the steps involved in planning advertising campaign.

Q2. (a) How does sales promotion supplement a firm's integrated marketing communication strategy? Explain with an example.

(b) What are the various types of media available for advertising? Discuss.

Q3. (a) Comment on the reach of Internet in India. Do you think it can affect the reach of traditional press and television as an advertising medium? Discuss with support your reasons.

(b) What is a social issue? Taking an example explain the various steps that one must consider to arrive at a strategy and to create communication material.

Q4. Write short notes on any three of the following:
(a) Illustration
(b) Copy testing
(c) Media Scheduling
(4) Direct mail
(e) Agency growth: Style and content

Section—B

Q5. (a) A local furniture company targets college students and working professionals with accommodation of young people purchasing their first furniture items. What type of media would you use for advertising campaign? Propose and justify giving reasons.

(b) Advertising is a very important marketing tool. What does sales promotion accomplish that advertising cannot for:

(i) A retailer

(ii) Manufacturer

Management of Marketing Communication and Advertising: MS-68
February, 2021

Note: (i) Attempt any three questions from Section A, Section B is compulsory.
(ii) All questions carry equal marks.

Section—A

Q1. (a) What is marketing communication? Discuss the role of marketing communication in bringing the marketer and consumer close together to achieve the marketing objectives.

(b) Discuss the Personality factors affecting consumer buying decisions in the following situations:
(i) Online buying
(ii) Insurance

Q2. (a) Distinguish between creative ideas and creative associations, giving suitable examples.

(b) Explain the various kinds of creative associations in advertising, giving suitable examples.

Q3. (a) With the help of suitable examples, discuss the objectives of sales promotion.

(b) What do you understand by "positioning"? What are the positioning alternatives available for advertising a brand? Explain with an example.

Q4. Write short notes on any three of the following:
(a) Consumer Perception
(b) Message Presentation
(c) Measuring Recall
(d) Characteristics of TV vs Radio
(e) Functions of Advertising Agency

Section—B

Q5. Read the following case carefully and answer the questions given at the end:

ICT the tobacco-to-hotels major has changed the identity of its lifestyle apparel brand from Thrills Lifestyle to WLS. It will now sell apparel that is 100% natural — from fabric to threads, buttons and labels. Having made it all natural, it had introduced a sharp differentiator in the apparel market riding on the current bandwagon of preference for natural and organic products. It has become the first mainstream Indian apparel brand to go natural.

By renaming its premium apparel retail brand to WLS, it has effectively removed the brand's connection with the Thrills cigarette brand and made the brand name small, simple and trendier, in line with other brands like AJIO, M&S and D&G.

However, it remains to be seen how much impact rebranding will have on the prospects of ICT's lifestyle retailing business. The segment has been under pressure in recent years — effectively pulling down the growth rates of the company's FMCG business. According to the latest annual report, 2017-18, it was another challenging year for the branded apparel segment. On the contrary, e-commerce players continued with their aggressive push to capture market share amongst value seeking consumers by offering heavy discounts and launching exclusive labels and brands.

Merely rebranding alone may not help the company unless combined with change in marketing communication strategy and execution. Although this rebranding will help to some extent, still the company needs to take more steps to get back strong growth in this business. The tectonic shift comes at a time when consumers are increasingly becoming conscious of their impact on environment.

Questions:

(a) Was rebranding their apparel business the right decision? Justify your answer.

(b) Propose an integrated marketing communication mix strategy for the rebranded apparel business of the company.

❑❑❑

Management of Marketing Communication and Advertising: MS-68

June, 2021

Note: (i) Answer any three questions from Section A. (ii) Section B is compulsory. (iii) All questions carry equal marks.

Section—A

Q1. (a) Explain the various steps involved in developing a promotion strategy.
(b) Develop a promotion strategy for a DTH service provider.

Q2. (a) Explain the various types of mass media available to an advertiser and evaluate their merits and demerits.
(b) Why is it necessary to measure the effectiveness of an advertising campaign? Discuss with an example.

Q3. (a) Distinguish between advertising research and marketing research, giving suitable examples.
(b) What is direct marketing? Discuss its advantages and limitations.

Q4. Write short notes on any three of the following:
(a) Rural media scene
(b) Headline
(c) Syndicated and custom research techniques
(d) Ethical issues in advertising
(e) Media strategy

Section—B

Q5. A few decades ago Green Revolution initiatives had transformed Indian Agriculture sector in terms of quality, productivity and sustenance.

But today, any product/service offered with a tag 'GREEN' i.e. by prefixing has very few takers (for various reasons) yet the curiosity to know more about such offerings is remarkable. Taking a cue a Marketing Manager of a Green tea brand wishes to organise a consumer contest for creating better awareness and enhance the popularity of said brand. The Manager is primarily concerned to get inputs from rural and semi urban markets and also more inputs from the urban areas as well.

Questions:

(a) Suggest the details of the consumer contest covering the following:

(i) Theme for the contest

(ii) Duration of the contest and closing data

(iii) Prises to be offered

(iv) Judgment criteria

(v) Any other you may wish is relevant can be included

(b) What would you advise the Manager to do to evaluate the effectiveness of the contest?

Management of Marketing Communication and Advertising: MS-68
December, 2021

Note: (i) Answer any three questions from Section A. (ii) Section B is compulsory. (iii) All questions carry equal marks.

Section—A

Q1. (a) Explain the role of marketing communication in achieving a firm's marketing goals.
(b) Briefly discuss the consumer variables that are relevant in designing marketing communication.

Q2. (a) Explain with a suitable example the steps involved in developing a promotion strategy.
(b) Define the concept of creativity. What are the alternatives available to a creative director for creative associations of a footwear brand?

Q3. (a) Discuss the four basic elements of media strategy for a jewellery brand.
(b) Discuss the meaning and scope of direct marketing in the current scenario.

Q4. Write short notes on any three of the following:
(a) Rural Media Options
(b) Syndicated and Custom Research Technique
(c) Managing Sales Promotion in Service Marketing
(d) Popular Agency Structure
(e) Ethics in Advertising

Section—B

Q5. Read the following case carefully and answer the questions given at the end:

A small sised north-based FMCG company has forayed into wheat flour (Atta) as a new product offering with a brand name "Desi Atta" which was launched in Jan 2020. The brand was conceived targeting the middle and lower middle class homemakers of the northern belt. The Atta brand is priced much lower than its competitors and yet it claims that the quality and packaging is at par with the market leader.

Just two months after its launch, a lockdown was declared due to COVID-19 and as a result the firm was constrained to undertake any kind of promotional effort. However, the top management is now of the opinion that the brand needs to be advertised strategically in creating awareness and visibility as a short/medium-term impact on sales and brand recall.

In view of being a small company and the focus of selective market coverage, it was decided that the marketing department, which is strong enough and well-equipped with a couple of seasoned managers, should initiate and undertake the task of advertising by preparing a comprehensive advertising plan for the next 3 years.

Questions:

(a) List the possible advertising objectives for the brand.

(b) Discuss the suitable Integrated Marketing Communication (IMC) for the proposed brand of wheat flour (Atta).

(c) Suggest suitable media selection and the choice of media mix decisions for the brand.